A Vocation at Risk

A Vocation at Risk

A Survival Guide for New Teachers

James A. Bryant Jr.

ROWMAN & LITTLEFIELD
Lanham • Boulder • New York • London

Published by Rowman & Littlefield
An imprint of The Rowman & Littlefield Publishing Group, Inc.
4501 Forbes Boulevard, Suite 200, Lanham, Maryland 20706
www.rowman.com

6 Tinworth Street, London SE11 5AL, United Kingdom

Copyright © 2021 by James A. Bryant Jr.

All rights reserved. No part of this book may be reproduced in any form or by any electronic or mechanical means, including information storage and retrieval systems, without written permission from the publisher, except by a reviewer who may quote passages in a review.

British Library Cataloguing in Publication Information Available

Library of Congress Cataloging-in-Publication Data Available

ISBN 978-1-4758-5855-6 (cloth)
ISBN 978-1-4758-5856-3 (pbk.)
ISBN 978-1-4758-5857-0 (electronic)

For my students—the future teachers of America, and the guarantors and guardians of this fragile democracy.

I do not promise you ease. I do not promise you comfort. But I do promise you these: hardship, weariness, and suffering.

And with them, I promise you victory.

—Garibaldi

On the education of children depends the future of nations.

—Hazrat Inayat Khan

Contents

	Foreword: The Faith of a Teacher	xi
	Introduction	1
Chapter 1	Forever Unfit to be a Slave	5
Chapter 2	Pilgrims to the Horizon	19
Chapter 3	Rowing to Galveston	33
Chapter 4	Standing on Desks	47
Chapter 5	The Same River Twice	59
Chapter 6	"Well Done, Young Man"	75
Chapter 7	Dispatch from the Jericho Road	91
Chapter 8	Issues and Trends	107
Chapter 9	A Vocation at Risk: Outflanking the Forty-eight	121
	Bibliography	131

Foreword

The Faith of a Teacher

I don't recall wanting to be a teacher when I was a young girl. Flight attendant or veterinarian, yes, but not a teacher. I had never flown on a commercial plane as a youngster, and we didn't take our animals to the vet much, but those professions seemed bigger than life to my younger self. My sister, whose goal was to be a veterinarian, and I spent a majority of our time, though, playing school. One of us was the teacher, the other was the student. Any friends or cousins who were visiting had to join the class. We had acquired some old textbooks, we had a small chalkboard, and we had plenty of paper and pens/pencils, so we were good to go.

My father, an educator himself, encouraged both my sister and me as we began seriously considering our futures to earn our teaching credentials, regardless of our majors. He said, "You never know when you may need your teaching license." We appreciated the advice, but education still did not seem like a viable major for me when I began college. I started with business, shifted to pre-pharmacy, and landed on writing and editing for a while. Life circumstances led me to begin substitute teaching one spring semester at the high school I attended and where I am now the principal, and I was hooked, so to speak. I changed my major, and twenty-seven years later, I am still in education.

I knew my "why" then, and I know my "why" today, and while I've added to it, the fundamental "I want to make a difference" is still at the heart of all I do. What I did not have when starting out in my own classroom for the very first time was a *Survival Guide for Beginning Teachers*, a resource that encourages new teachers to know their "why," to embrace the noble profession of teaching, and to be aware of the difficulties and challenges that lie ahead.

This *Survival Guide* is not a "cookbook method of teaching." Instead, this book guides us through the role of education—what it was, is, and should be—and the role of teachers in the learning process, as co-learners, as communicators, as transformers. It explores teaching as it is connected to and influenced by administration, and as it is both ideological and political.

When I return to my "why" daily, I am reminded of "the inherent individuality of each and every student who crosses the threshold of our classroom doors," and I am encouraged to promote the education of each of these individuals with the energy, fervor, and creativity necessary to meet them where they are, level the playing field, and send them on to their futures prepared. This is possible through the faith of teachers. We have to believe that we can make a difference. We have to believe that our students are individuals. We have to believe that we can meet their unique educational needs. We have to believe that getting to know our students is vital.

This *Survival Guide*, while written to support new teachers, is a wonderful support for veteran teachers as well. It is a reminder that "the faith of a teacher can make all the difference—an important reason we must stay vigilant against becoming cynics and abandoning hope in our profession. There is too much at stake for us to give in."

For me the *Survival Guide* helped me to realize that the profession of teaching is bigger than life, and I am thankful this profession chose me.

Dr. Deborah Kinsland Foerst
Principal, Cherokee High School
Cherokee, North Carolina

Introduction

George Bernard Shaw once opined, "Those who can, do. Those who can't, teach." The true intent of the phrase has been debated since it appeared for more than a century ago as a line in Man and Superman, a play authored by Shaw. Allow me to humbly put the debate to rest. To have the audacity to believe, let alone say, that those who can't, teach, is, without question . . . *the truth*. It is the absolute truth. Those who have answered the call to teach, as Shaw and thousands of others have remarked in the century since, in fact, "can't."

Educators *can't* sit idly by when the work they do every single moment of each day matters beyond measure. Despite the criticism, the lack of funding, the nearly nonexistent support, and the stark reality that the field of education seems to be under constant attack, teachers continue to show up day after day, impacting the lives of their students in immeasurable and invaluable ways. Futures are shaped and saved all across this country, and around the globe, when teachers decide they can't.

Educators *can't* allow the cycles of the past to remain unbroken. For some of our youth, their *only* chance to break the repetitive, generational cycles of racism, sexism, poverty, and ignorance is a teacher who can't—and won't—accept that these cycles are immutable. The pattern of settling for a journey down familiar roads instead of roads never traveled is one that a dedicated teacher will find unacceptable. The educator who takes a keen interest in the "troubled kid" in the back of the class who, previously, had only been seen in a negative light, dares destiny. A seemingly forgotten child is no longer invisible. That is compassion and investment, whether it be social, emotional, mental, academic, or a combination of these. For some, that is all it takes to begin breaking the vicious cycle that would otherwise have remained unbroken. A life's course altered forever because a teacher decided she can't.

With investment comes advocacy, another can't. Educators *can't* allow those under their tutelage and care to go without appropriate advocacy. Many of our children do not have the capability or wherewithal to speak up for themselves. Enter their teachers. The voices of the voiceless. Voices that *will* be heard, because educators cannot remain silent. Don't make us use our "teacher's voice," because we *can't* do so quietly and we *will* voice whatever is heavy on our hearts in an unapologetic fashion.

We use those teachers' voices to vocalize concerns and highlight issues that often go ignored and unmentioned. We use those voices to send messages loudly, clearly, and with authority in the arenas of politics and policy. This is not about reds or blues or parties. The *only* party a teacher belongs to is the one of moral high ground that places the best interests of youth at the forefront. They are our constituents, and our work for the betterment of their lives is never done. The youth are the future, our greatest resource, and the future is in your classroom, in your hands. Like those before them, they will play a vital role in the history of their generation, and the history that is written will reflect some part of your influence on those history makers.

Robert F. Kennedy spoke of history by saying,

> history will judge you, and as the years pass, you will ultimately judge yourself, in the extent to which you have used your gifts and talents to lighten and enrich the lives of your fellow men. In your hands lies the future of your world and the fulfillment of the best qualities of your own spirit.

So, I ask, how will you enrich the lives of others with the great responsibility placed before you? What qualities of your own spirit do you want to impart on those around you? Will you judge yourself proudly at the end of your life's work? The answers to each of these questions are within your control.

To have a heart for bestowing knowledge to others is one of the most selfless acts one can participate in. To do so is to share and, in essence, give up part of yourself to others. The teaching profession is, indeed, noble and selfless. We impart knowledge with the hope that we can make our world a little bit better both while we are here and long after we are gone as our influence continues to be felt through the lives of those we are blessed to impact in some small manner along the way. This legacy makes every obstacle and challenge placed before us worth it. It also makes overcoming and conquering every obstacle and every challenge a crucial venture.

Make no mistake. The critics will always be there and they will let you know of their presence. Despite that, you cannot compromise your convictions. After all, you have answered the call, and you were called for a reason. You were chosen. Never forget that or lose sight of "the compelling why"—the children.

Dedicate yourself to holding steadfast in doing all that you *can*, even when you are told you *can't*. Drown out the noise and stay the course.

Regardless of what others may say, and how much will be said, believe that you *can*.

When you are praised, believe that you *can*. When you are criticized, believe that you *can*.

Even when you feel like you *can't*, believe that you *can*.

Follow what you know is right in your heart.

Refuse to give up in the face of adversity.

Promote awareness for the issues most threatening our country, which are likely adversely affecting the youth in your classroom.

Find others who will lift you up and find some way to lift up others in every chance you get.

Keep the faith and have a hopeful heart.

Understanding, compassion, and kindness are key.

Lead with love.

Never hesitate to get into "good trouble."

Remain persistent in the pursuit of achieving the impossible.

Believe in your own magic and make it happen.

Believe in the differences that you can make, that you *will* make. Believe in a better today and a better tomorrow because of the inspiration and wisdom you provide. Believe in our young folks. Believe in yourself. At this very moment, someone out there is counting on you. You may already know them. They may be occupying a seat in your classroom right now. You may not even know they exist yet. Regardless, they are counting on you. You *can't* let them down, and you won't, because you *can*. History needs you, and it is counting on you, too.

Cody A. Beasley
Elementary school teacher

CHAPTER 1

∼

Forever Unfit to be a Slave

Know this: as a teacher you *will* have a legacy. You *will* make a difference in the life of a child. By sheer virtue of the amount of time you spend with your students you will make an impact. On that you have no say. What *is* up to you is the kind of difference you make, the kind of legacy you will create. Consider the example of one Mr. Ostrowski, an English teacher. Ostrowski's words and examples were recalled by one of his students a quarter century after being in his class. The young man dreamed of becoming a lawyer, and Mr. Ostrowski provided him with inspiration of a sort.

"You've got to be realistic about being a nigger," he told his student,

> A lawyer—that's no realistic goal for a nigger. You need to think about something you *can* be. You're good with your hands—making things. Everybody admires your carpentry shop work. Why don't you plan on carpentry?[1]

Following this incident the student's "grades plummeted and his truculence increased. Within several months, [the student] found himself expelled."[2] Near the end of his life, the student, Malcolm X., still recalled the painful sting of his teacher's words. In his fourth decade Malcolm X., who by then was an international figure of some renown and respect, was still haunted by the moment. To be sure, that is a legacy.

Or, consider the example of James D. Kennedy, the former US history and drama teacher at West Stanly High School in Oakboro, North Carolina. Mr. Kennedy founded the West Stanly Players, a noted dramatics club that had a reputation as one of the finest in North Carolina. He retired from teaching in 1997, turning the reins of his beloved program over to a former student. In 2001, in honor of the thirtieth anniversary of the Players' founding,

Kennedy's students gathered from across the country and returned to the theater he once prowled to dedicate a bronze plaque in his honor.

An interview with Mr. Kennedy served as the final class in a course called the Legacy Project, designed not to look at the mechanics of education, but rather at the role of social consciousness within the classroom and taught at the University of North Dakota. As the hour drew to a close, one of the students asked Mr. Kennedy for his own, personal definition of "teaching." What had it meant to him? Mr. Kennedy paused only briefly before answering. "Education," he said, "is a dialogue with humanity."[3] Mr. Kennedy advised the pre-service teachers that this dialogue of which he spoke had as its foundation a teacher's altruism and humanism—in other words a teacher's own social consciousness and sense of societal responsibility.

"Teaching is, no more and no less, than a moral endeavor," he said.[4] "I mean, Jesus was a teacher. So was Confucius and Mohammed. You can't find much better company than that."[5] That afternoon, as the students sat around the large, rectangular table in the dean's conference room, their eyes filled with anxiety and excitement, Mr. Kennedy did not exhort them to master any particular content—though he would have assumed such intellectual rigor.

Kennedy concluded,

> When my head hits the pillow at night . . . I am happy that my life's work was spent doing right by my fellow man. Always remember that when you are in that classroom, you are dealing with our most precious natural resource. I got a call recently from an old student who is now in prison, and he wanted to call and tell me that he thought of me often, and that he was determined to get his life back on track because he knew that I had believed he could be something.[6]

Before ending our call he urged them—and me—to focus on the big picture of teaching—to focus on the *why*.

It is time for teachers at all levels of our educational establishment to reclaim the conversations about education by demanding that we talk about the fundamentals of education. It is time for educators to take back the language and the discussions around this profession by focusing again on the basic *why* of education, the fundamental *why* that inspired us to become teachers in the first place. It is time schools of education—specifically teacher preparation programs—return to talking about BIG ideas—foundational principles for education in a democratic society, the moral, political, ethical, and professional demands of being in a profession that is on the frontlines of the constant struggle to preserve this republic.

We can and must no longer accept schools of education offering a petty curriculum—focused on nuts and bolts at the exclusion of principles and dispositions. Maxine Greene defined teaching as "purposeful action," and we should remember that those purposes must be more than the mere transmission of a set of facts.[7] Successful teachers are never small—they hold a horizon encompassing view of their profession and have a crusading spirit of compassion and inquiry. We need schools of education infused with Alfred North Whitehead's romance and wonder, not bogged down in standards written by men and women whose true purpose is anathema to genuine educators.

Helen McKenna, a high school science teacher of twenty-one years, spoke eloquently to Ray Raphael of her view of what being a teacher meant to her. "If I did quit teaching," she said,

> I'm not really sure what else I'd get involved in. What are you going to do in society that's meaningful? And I do believe in meaningful work. Working with kids in the public schools is a very meaningful job in our society. One of the only ones.[8]

Good teaching requires students to consider big questions and wrestle with difficult, often painful issues. These are the questions and the principles that made me—an accidental teacher—a lifelong teacher.

I was hired to teach tenth-grade US history in 1996 and my plan was to teach one year, save some money, and head off to law school. My passion for history got in the way of those plans, however. My passion for students ended any thought of law school. I was both drawn to and concerned by the challenge posed by being a high school history teacher. I found that my students all showed up on that first day of class expecting I would be the worst hour of their day. They expected that because, simply put, that's what "social studies" had usually been to them. It didn't take long to see why.

The books were dry to read and often wrong. The exercises that they were used to—color maps, doing crossword puzzles, and word searches—left them bored almost to tears. We had reduced history to a series of atrocities and glories, all of which were presented as somehow preordained. There was no element of human drama. I became determined to pursue a degree that would allow me to work with future history teachers and, hopefully, make a difference in the way our nation's story was presented to our nation's young people.

Having had no prior education courses, but having the experience of four years inside the classroom, I assumed I had a pretty good idea of what teachers were being trained for and what they were being taught. I was wrong. Massive amounts of time were dedicated to things that were trivial at best, and some of the most vital information that young teachers should be given were ignored completely.

It was no wonder there was such a desperate turnover rate among new teachers. They were getting out into the field and finding that their training was, in many ways, worthless. Many of the things a new teacher faces that are the most trying and troublesome are not broached at all in teacher preparation courses, leaving teachers unprepared for their classrooms.

The most glaring failure of schools of education is the obsession with the technical aspects of teaching. The art of education is shuttled rudely under a rug to make room for more practice at developing a thorough lesson plan, or a "professional portfolio" that, in all likelihood, will never be opened again once these future teachers gain employment. William Ayers wrote, "Students of teaching spend an inordinate amount of time learning how to make lesson plans (an astonishingly simple, entirely overblown, and not very useful skill), or reading the research in classroom management."[9]

Course after course in education programs ask future teachers to develop a lesson plan, many if not most of which they are never given the opportunity to actually teach. Reams of paper are expended on lessons developed for hypothetical students in fictional classrooms. By the time students of education were ready to graduate, they had the format of these plans memorized.

The problem is the obvious disconnect between what pre-service teachers are being trained to do and what they will actually do once in the field. We are fooling ourselves if we don't think they are hearing acidic complaints about teacher preparation from their cooperating teachers in the field. Veteran teachers take one look at these absurd lesson plan forms—page after mind-numbing page—and get a healthy laugh out of them.

They know, as will our student teachers soon enough, that such a form is a waste. This is not because teachers are lazy or don't care about putting together an effective lesson. It is because, in the myriad of responsibilities a teacher must face from day to day, no time is left for such beautiful and detailed plans.

Planning periods are a rush of meetings and returned phone calls. After school is spent monitoring detention or saddled with bus duty, and then maybe tutoring a student or two. Home is a blur of grabbing some rest, grading papers, spending time with family, or other personal pursuits and responsibilities. A teacher may face over one hundred papers to grade, ranging from quizzes to term papers. Once all that is done, usually around midnight, no one wants to trudge to the computer and write out objectives, goals, purposes, materials, and so on. The vast majority of teachers I know write their lesson plans in one to two paragraphs that make no sense to anyone but themselves, written in some form of personal Sanskrit.

Moreover, the ability to write one of these Dickensian plans does not mean that a teacher can actually *teach* it. Let's face it, *Death of a Salesman* is a great and moving play, but you wouldn't know it based on the tortuous high school productions inflicted on parents and other relatives each and every spring across the country. The plan is only as good as the performance. We lie to future teachers when we reduce their thoughts about teaching to such a narrow, introspective process.

Teaching is the ultimate extroverted activity—it is all about those around us and under our care. To write a good speech is not, necessarily, to be a good speaker. That is why there was a President Kennedy but not a President Sorenson. A lovely plan on pretty paper with cute little clipart around the edges means nothing unless it translates into good teaching. Can we possibly imagine a culinary college teaching its students to write recipes at the expense of having them cook?

Future teachers can also expect in their preparation programs to be exposed to (much like a virus) the cause *du jour* in education these days, whatever that cause may be. Only pop music is more fad-driven than education. The particular fad will change, but rest assured there will be something—some one-size-fits-all answer—with which education becomes fully enamored. For a few years, it was the professional portfolio. A waste of time significantly beneath the intellectual level of most college students, the professional portfolio was better suited for middle school children than seniors in a university setting.

The critiques of student portfolios were often laughable at best, tragic at worst. Students spent hours upon hours filling notebooks with their old papers (called "reflections"), elaborate cover sheets and, of course, lesson plans. God knows how many trees sacrificed their lives so that students can relate how many different standards they can meet in a single reflection. These standards range from National Council for Accreditation of Teacher Education, federal, state, and local standards, which most professors profess not to like but still gamely insist on having thoroughly addressed by students. These standards are the educational equivalent of one's personal horoscope—written in such jargon-laden obtuseness as to allow the pre-service teacher to make them mean whatever they need them to mean in order to fill the portfolio.

More ominously, drowning in this vapid minutia, far too many teacher preparation programs utterly fail to remind students of the deeply moral and ethical nature of the teaching profession. This failure is a theme of much of what Harvard educator Vito Perrone has written. In his book *A Letter to Teachers: Reflections on Schooling and the Art of Teaching*, Perrone writes, "Turning teachers into technicians, intermediaries for someone else's ideas and curriculum . . . [is] very poor policy."[10] This poor policy often serves to drive teachers away from the profession.

What keeps those who stay from leaving is often answered by acknowledging the idealism and commitment of those teachers, their sense of social responsibility and consciousness. They understand, honor, and perhaps even crave that dialogue with humanity of which Mr. Kennedy spoke. Paulo Freire writes about the integral role education plays in the building of true democracy: "Democracy, like any dream, is not made with spiritual words but with reflection and practice. It is not what I say that says I am a democrat, that I am not racist or machista, but what I do."[11] Thus, we see teaching described as a worthy societal function, vocation, guardian of democracy, and moral exemplar.

Recalling the words of Dr. Perrone, however, we are still confronted with the concern that pre-service teachers are not being adequately prepared for these diverse functions and roles. This concern is borne out by a study done at Boston University by Malinda Jane Wells in 1998. She wrote, "Studies have shown that although teachers find that their job requires them to engage in moral education on a day-to-day basis, they received little or no preparation for this task in their preservice teacher training programs."[12] While many teacher preparation programs are attempting to integrate elements of social consciousness, idealism, and moral education into their different course offerings, the connections are not self-evident to our students and are too often being missed entirely.

Myles Horton wrote in his introduction to William Ayers's *To Teach: The Journey of a Teacher* that "all education is a form of social action based on some kind of social philosophy."[13] Earl V. Pullias and James D. Young write that

> a distinguished psychologist once said that there are three roles no sensible person should undertake: parent, statesman, or teacher. The relationships are so complex and often contradictory, the demands so inescapable, the stakes so high that a thoughtful person has a natural tendency to pull back from the responsibilities.[14]

Those who do not "pull back"—our pre-service teachers—do so from a sense of civic duty or social consciousness.

More must be done to foster and cultivate these ideals in our programs. Too often self-conscious and intellectually insecure, our programs are kept from this important work because educators have tried to define ourselves in ways more pleasing to our brethren in the academy, turning steadfastly and stubbornly away from the more humanistic and idealistic elements of teaching and trying to quantify a job that will never lend itself to cold, clinical analysis.

The failure with this paradigm becomes apparent when we consider Parker Palmer's description of the fundamental function of a teacher: "Teachers must . . . create emotional space in the classroom, space that allows feelings to arise and be dealt with."[15] This creation of a safe emotional plane for students is something many teachers will do well naturally, but it is also something with which many future teachers will need help, and this is a skill set that cannot be reduced to a rubric. Ignoring these topics is dangerous, for teachers will without question need these emotional skills to succeed.

This is not, to be sure, a call for a purely emotive program of training teachers or what some might deride as a curriculum of fluff. The tension that arises between curriculums designed to allow pre-service teachers to concentrate on the moral, spiritual, emotional, and social implications of their work and the knowledge needed for content purposes is really no more than a false choice.

Palmer notes this tension and labels the competing schools of thought "scholars" versus "student-centered folks."[16] He does not, however, allow these labels to stand as definite, permanent schisms in the field of education. He argues such "professors were not debating teaching techniques [but] . . . were revealing the diversity of identity and integrity among themselves."[17]

Hansen agreed with this idea, writing that teachers "enact their sense of service in strikingly different ways. That fact suggests that it may be more useful to speak of the 'senses' of a vocation than it is to reach for a single, unified definition."[18] These authors are not promoting a theory or framework of teacher education that places little or no emphasis on knowledge of and proficiency in a certain subject matter or a mastering of content knowledge. Rather, they show the desperate need to understand that this knowledge and proficiency is but one aspect of teaching.

One tragic outcome of this great turning away from the moral and ethical foundations of teaching has been our surrender of the language of education. The result for our students is a lexicon that does not inspire but leaves them frustrated and cold. One obvious example is the word "praxis." A quick Google search of the term "the meaning of practice" is a useful, if depressing, exercise. The second item that appears is the Oxford dictionary definition: *practice, as distinguished from theory*. A noun, *praxis*, is also described as "the gap between theory and practice" and clearly implies informed, purposeful *action*.

But the word has a new and insidious meaning for future teachers, as is seen by the very first item that Google spits out for this particular search. Before the definition, the seeker is sent to a site that promises test preparation and tips for another version of praxis—a standardized test foisted upon future teachers. Praxis now means nothing more to them than a standardized test they must survive in order to collect a paycheck. The irony here would be extremely satisfying if it were not so very sad. To be sure, taking an exam is an action. The process of filling in ovals completely and without going outside the lines is an action. Where, however, is the reflection? It does not exist.

Despite the relative discomfort among many professional educators with standardized testing, there has been an acquiescence to using this test as a doorkeeper to the classroom. Our intellectual insecurity comes into play here, too. This test, along with the abomination of EdTPA, is now serving as our version of the bar exam—showing the world that we are serious about standards and accountability. What it really shows, however, is that we lack the courage of our convictions.

We tell our students that we see great peril in the "No Child Left Behind" plan to test every child from second through eighth grade, but we require them to take a similar test. There are massive complaints about "Race to the Top" and its reductive approach to understanding schools and communities through testing, and yet we sit idly by as states impose standardized tests on our students, insulting our competence and their achievement. The hypocrisy is not lost on future teachers, who will, as a result, be less likely to stand fast against the testing phenomenon in their own districts and states.

An equally powerful example of this jargon-practice disconnect is the word "pedagogy." This is a term bandied about all the time in our classes and our programs, and yet there is a painful dearth of understanding about what this word actually means. I make it a habit of asking my students how many of them have heard this word, and then ask them to define it for me. The answers are always the same.

"Teaching methods," they will say proudly, happy that they have retained something in their time with us. "Teaching strategies" is another popular response. So is "ways of teaching." The most Orwellian answer is, "The science of teaching." All of the responses show a belief that the word describes some group of activities or theories that can be utilized in the classroom—a cookbook approach to education.

Donaldo Macedo gives us another view into the meaning of this word in his introduction to the classic *Pedagogy of the Oppressed*. In it, we learn that pedagogy "has Greek roots, meaning 'to lead a child' (from *pays*: child and *ago*: to lead). Thus, as the term 'pedagogy' illustrates, education is inherently directive and must always be transformative."[19] Perhaps we avoid this definition because we fear it places too great a burden on young (or veteran) teachers. Claiming that education "must always be transformative" demands that our lesson plans challenge and cajole, that our work in the classroom be nothing short of revolutionary.

Vito Perrone writes, "We need educational settings that challenge young people intellectually and morally."[20] Such educational settings would demand our students to prepare for democracy by practicing it. This is a radical demand, and one that many politicians would no doubt be very uncomfortable swallowing. It also becomes apparent through this definition of every educator's favorite word that there can never be a one-size-fits-all methodology of education. If our classrooms are to be directive and transformative, then we have to recognize the inherent individuality of each and every student who crosses the threshold of our classroom doors.

Driven by our fears of not being taken seriously by other professionals, we are seeking generalizations and replication. The search for that Grand Theory of Education that can be translated across cultures and generations is futile at best and destructive at worst. It is as worthless as the efforts to design a standardized test that is fair to all people, all cultures, and both genders.

If we want our students to learn, then we must move away from this need for a theory or method that will reach the masses and understand that all education is an individualistic exercise and therefore must be geared toward the individual. We must stop seeing data and once again see the child's right in front of us. This is a professional, ethical, and moral imperative.

We cannot answer the demand of pedagogy and transform our students unless we know their needs as individuals and do not assume their needs as a race or class or gender. And yet what we have allowed the word to become—teaching methods—would lead us to believe that there is, in fact, a generic student who can be reached if we commit the right theories to memory. The result has been a factory mentality in education, with children coming down the conveyor belt just waiting for the right "part" to be added so that they may become productive and successful citizens.

Robert F. Kennedy was fond of quoting the Greek classicist Edith Hamilton's critique of American education:

> One critic [of America's educational system] has said, "Education [is] by its very nature an individual matter . . . not geared to mass production. It does not produce people who instinctively go the same way . . . [yet] our millions learn the same lessons and spend hours before television sets looking at exactly

the same thing at exactly the same time. For one reason and another we are more and more ignoring differences, if not trying to obliterate them. We seem headed toward a standardization of the mind, what Goethe called 'the deadly commonplace that fetter us all'"[21]

This is exactly the point made over and again by our loss of the power of educational language.

If pedagogy means "to lead a child," then we should instinctively understand that, as Hamilton pointed out so eloquently, all children will not be led to the same place, to the same endpoint. If praxis truly means "action with reflection" then we intuitively know that, upon reflection, different decisions and opinions will be reached according to the backgrounds, biases, and lives of our students.

Our pedagogy must become that most revolutionary of practices—providing our students with the means to question all they see around them, the ability to come to their own conclusions about this world and their place and role in it. Constructivist philosophy argues that our students should engage in the process of utilizing their knowledge and constructing their own values and ethics, and as John Dewey pointed out throughout his life, this construction begins on the individual foundation that students bring with them from home and from life.

Ivan Illich argues that "the mere existence of school discourages and disables the poor from taking control of their own learning."[22] One could argue that this is not only true for the poor but for all children engaged in an educational system that portends a one-size-fits-all mentality. By confusing "to lead a child" with "successful teaching strategies," we send the message that there is one "answer" to which we lead children. This answer is typically the paradigm of a materialistic society in which corporations and politicians define learning as assimilating into the status quo.

Even in Jane Addams' day, there was a disconnect between the good life shown in "the house of dreams" on the stage and the reality in the ghettoes.[23] Addams pointed out that this disconnect, like the television dreams mentioned by Hamilton, caused frustration and bitterness among the youth of her Chicago neighborhood. When Illich argues that we discourage learning, he understands that our young are not fooled by our comfortable platitudes that claim every problem has an easy answer and that every controversy leads to a singular conclusion.

Their own experiences, which we shut out of the debate with our standardization of the mind, tell them this is not so. We ignore the important lesson from Parker Palmer, who wrote, "Hospitality in the classroom requires not only that we treat our students with civility and compassion but also that we invite our students and their insights into the conversation."[24] Each time we deny the lived experience of a student and demand subservience to the gossamer lies of the establishment, we do incalculable damage to our democracy.

Perhaps we are afraid that if we lead our students to a questioning pose, they will find us to be the charlatans we ourselves fear we have become. If we cannot offer future teachers a model of teaching that will work in every classroom, then why do our departments even exist? Fearful of what lies ahead, our students want to know what and how to teach, and we willingly oblige them. We must overcome this fear eating away at our ability to tell our students the truth: there is no cookbook method of teaching that will always be there to save them.

The best we can do is instill in our future teachers' compassion for the individual attributes of this profession. The truth is that leading a child means knowing when to teach, and when to get out of the way. The truth is that pedagogy means cultivating opinions, and it emphatically does not mean providing them. We must—again and again—return to the foundational principles and ethics that sustain us.

Taking back the language of education is nothing less than a revolutionary ideal. Perrone offers a dire warning about this curriculum of minutiae we have allowed to capture our schools of education: "When large purposes lose their centrality, schools tend to drift, forfeiting their independence and their educational and social power."[25] The words matter because they remind us of our large purposes and because they provide this profession, which we all love so much, with its voice. We must not forget or belittle the fact that every true, meaningful revolution begins with words.

Revolutions are born in the minds of the thinker, and are then committed to paper. Finally, these words spring to life in the streets. Edith Hamilton wrote, "All things are at odds when God sets a thinker loose on the planet."[26] It is a teacher's duty to give God an assist in the creation of thinkers, questioners, and seekers. It is, in fact, our calling. History teaches us that language has established faiths and doomed governments. We must begin immediately the work of reclaiming the vocabulary of education. We must reestablish the true meanings of words like pedagogy and praxis in our classrooms and in the hearts and minds of our students, who themselves are future teachers.

If the cool detachment of objectivity is replaced with the passionate fires of idealism, then so be it. Freedom to think and question and, ultimately, to believe in the creative potential and possibilities of the human spirit—this is our calling. Southern slaveowners were abundantly clear about the power of education to transform oppression into freedom. The Maryland man who owned Frederick Douglass excoriated his wife for teaching Douglass to read. In his autobiography, Douglass wrote:

> Very soon, after I went to live with Mr. and Mrs. Auld, she very kindly commenced to teach me the A,B,C. After I had learned this, she assisted me in learning to spell words of three or four letters. Just at this point of my progress, Mr. Auld found out what was going on, and at once forbade Mrs. Auld to instruct me further, telling her among other things, that it was unlawful, as well as unsafe, to teach a slave to read. To use his own words, further, he said, "If you give a nigger an inch, he will take an ell. A nigger should know nothing but to obey his master—to do as he is told to do. Learning would *spoil* the best nigger in the world. Now . . . if you teach that nigger (speaking of myself) how to read, there would be no keeping him. It would forever unfit him to be a slave."[27]

For Douglass, the racist bile from Auld ushered in a powerful epiphany: "I now understood what had been to me a most perplexing difficulty," he remembered, "to wit, the white man's power to enslave the black man. It was a grand achievement, and I prized it highly. From that moment, I understood the pathway from slavery to freedom."[28] *This* is how we must again view and define education, not the transmission of "marketable skills," but the all-important pathway from slavery to freedom. The words already exist.

David T. Hansen calls teaching a "vocation" and defines this term as "work that has social value and that provides enduring personal meaning"; the kind of meaning that keeps teachers such as Helen McKenna coming to work each Fall.[29] "Teaching is a social practice whose importance is unquestioned," Hansen writes, "even if what makes it important remains the subject of continued debate."[30]

With all this in mind, I have set out in this book to provide young teachers with a "survival guide" for their first few years. It is my hope that this book will provide for future and new teachers a look at many of the practical aspects that are ignored or given short shrift in too many teacher-training programs, as well as some of the theory that may be useful in the classroom.

It is my desire throughout to make these connections clear, so that praxis—in its fullest meaning—may be approached during the reading. Too many young teachers feel unprepared and uninspired by their training, so much so, in fact, that they last only a few years in the profession. In order to keep our teachers, we must prepare them realistically for what they will face in the classroom—not simply fill their minds with the jargon and pet theories of the moment, which make their way through the academy. While providing this "practical" training, we must also provide them with a useful theoretical foundation and remind the pre-service teachers in our care of the idealism that is inherent in leading our nation's young men and women.

There is no more vital or noble job in America than that of a teacher. There is also no more difficult or challenging. Those who choose to accept this challenge deserve the best training possible, and I hope this book will assist in that endeavor. We must rethink and, I believe, develop a new approach in the way we train our nation's educators. Currently, we are too susceptible to the fads of the moment, too enamored with the professional veneer we are given through the use of jargon and pseudo-scientific test results. We should think carefully about the words of Ralph Waldo Emerson, who warned us that

> the Gods we worship write their names on our faces be sure of that. And a man will worship something—have no doubt about that, either. He may think that his tribute is paid in secret in the dark recesses of his heart—but it will out. That which dominates will determine his life and character. *Therefore, it behooves us to be careful what we worship, for what we are worshipping, we are becoming.*[31]

A teacher education preparation program must provide students with the practical information they need to survive, the theoretical foundations to inform and support their daily decisions, and the idealistic reminders that will guide them during the "dark days of the soul" which accompany every profession. To do less is to become satisfied with mediocrity—a response and outcome that is simply unacceptable.

Notes

1. Malcolm X and Alex Haley, *The Autobiography of Malcolm X* (New York: Ballantine Books, 1965), p. 38.

2. Manning Marable, *Malcolm X: A Life of Reinvention* (New York: Viking, 2011), Loc 801 of 13916 Kindle Edition.

3. James D. Kennedy to Legacy Project class, Phone interview, May 2, 2002.

4. Personal correspondence, April 27, 2002.

5. Phone interview, May 2, 2002.

6. Phone interview, May 2, 2002.

7. Maxine Greene, *The Teacher as Stranger: Educational Philosophy for the Modern Age* (Belmont, CA: Wadsworth, 1973), pp. 69–70.

8. Ray Raphael, *The Teacher's Voice: A Sense of Who We Are* (Portsmouth, NH: Heinemann, 1985), p. 71.

9. William Ayers, *To Teach: The Journey of a Teacher* (New York: Teachers College Press, 1993), p. 10.

10. Vito Perrone, *A Letter to Teachers: Reflections on Schooling and the Art of Teaching* (San Francisco, CA: Jossey-Bass, 1991), p. 80.

11. Paulo Freire, *Teachers as Cultural Workers: Letters to those Who Dare Teach* (Boulder, CO: Westview, 1998), p. 67.

12. Melinda Jane Wells, *Teacher Educators' Conceptions of the Responsibility of Teachers as Moral Educators*. Unpublished doctoral dissertation, Boston University, 1998, dissertation abstract.

13. Myles Horton, "Introduction." In William Ayers, *To Teach: The Journey of a Teacher* (New York: Teachers College Press, 1993), p. ix.

14. Earl V. Pullias and James D. Young, *A Teacher Is Many Things* (Bloomington, IN: Indiana University Press, 1968), p. 5.

15. Parker Palmer, *The Courage to Teach: The Inner Landscape of a Teacher's Life* (San Francisco, CA: Jossey-Bass, 1998), p. 83.

16. Palmer, *Courage to Teach*, p. 12.

17. Palmer, *Courage to Teach*, p. 12.

18. David T. Hansen, *The Call to Teach* (New York: Teachers College Press, 1995), p. 16.

19. Donaldo Macedo, "Introduction." In Paulo Freire, *Pedagogy of the Oppressed* (New York: Continuum, 2000), p. 25.

20. Vito Perrone, *Lessons for New Teachers* (Boston, MA: McGraw Hill, 2000), p. 55.

21. Robert F. Kennedy, *Make Gentle the Life of this World: The Vision of Robert F. Kennedy*, Maxwell Taylor Kennedy, Ed. (New York: Harcourt, Brace and Company, 1998), pp. 90–91.

22. Ivan Illich, *Deschooling Society* (New York: Harper and Row, 1970), p. 8.

23. Jane Addams, *On Education* (London: Transaction Publishers, 2002), pp. 143–161.

24. Palmer, *The Courage to Teach*, p. 79.

25. Perrone, *A Letter to Teachers*, p. 1.

26. Edith Hamilton, *The Greek Way* (New York: W.W. Norton and Company, 1993), p. 28.

27. Frederick Douglass, *Narrative of the Life of Frederick Douglass, An American Slave* (Boston, MA: Bedford Books, 1993), p. 57.

28. Douglass, *Narrative*, p. 58.

29. Hansen, *The Call to Teach*, p. 9.

30. Hansen, *The Call to Teach*, p. 9.

31. *The Book of Uncommon Prayer*, Constance Pollock and Daniel Pollock, Eds. (Dallas, TX: Word Publishing, 1996), p. 61.

CHAPTER 2

Pilgrims to the Horizon

One does not read a Zora Neale Hurston novel; no, one holds the novel while it sings to you. Born on January 7, 1891, in Notasulga, Alabama, Hurston rose to prominence as an anthropologist and author, becoming one of the prominent voices of the Harlem Renaissance and one of the America's greatest authors. Her father John Hurston was a proud and ambitious man who moved his large family to central Florida, to the small town of Eatonville, to chase his dreams.

The town itself was an epiphany for John and would have a powerful influence on Zora; incorporated on August 15, 1887, Eatonville was, as Zora wrote later, "a pure Negro town—charter, mayor, council, town marshal and all."[1] John had learned about Eatonville by chance—an offhanded, passing remark by a fellow traveler about a town entirely run by African Americans. John was incredulous, demanding to know, "Who bosses it, den?"

"Dey bosses it deyself," he was told.

"You mean," John again clarified, "dey runnin' de town 'thout de white folks?" He was assured that was, indeed, the case.

"Ah sho wants tuh see dat sight," a stunned Hurston managed.[2]

His daughter grew up surrounded by such a sight, and whether it was Eatonville's example or genetic inclination (or both), Zora was a ferociously strong-willed, independent, curious, and questioning child. Once, she decided she had to unravel that greatest of childhood mysteries—what lay beyond her horizon.

She recruited a friend and they agreed to depart early the next day. That following morning, Zora waited and waited, but her friend never arrived. When she finally found her, Zora was distraught to discover her friend's courage had abandoned her and she was staying put. The horizon seemed so far away, after all, and what if they weren't home by supper?

She was also too adventurous for her family. "I was always asking and making myself a crow in a pigeon's nest," she recalled. "It was hard on my family and surroundings, and they in turn were hard on me."[3] Her grandmother and her father both chastised her constantly. Zora wrote, "My grandmother worried about my forward ways a great deal. She had known slavery and to her my brazenness was unthinkable."[4] Her father, too, she remembered, "predicted dire things for me. The white folks were not going to stand for it. I was going to be hung before I got grown."[5]

Zora did receive encouragement, though. First from her mother, who always "exhorted her children at every opportunity to 'jump at de sun.'"[6] Later, there were educators who mentored and inspired her. Her description of her English professor, Dwight O.W. Holmes, is all to which a teacher might aspire. Holmes, Hurston recalled, was "the man who was to give me the keys to certain things" and the most "dynamic teacher anywhere under any skin."[7]

In her inimitable style she wrote:

> He radiates newness and nerve and says to your mind, 'There is something wonderful to behold just ahead. Let's go see what it is.' He is a pilgrim to the horizon. . . . He made the way clear. Something about his face killed the drabness and discouragement in me. I felt that the thing could be done.[8]

What a marvelous epitaph for any teacher—*she made me feel the thing could be done.*

Tommy Bell's first-grade teacher was less inspiring, unfortunately. Bell was born in Jamaica and moved along with his parents and nine siblings to West Philadelphia in 1947. That afternoon in first grade Tommy was deep in his own head—listening to the symphony playing there. His teacher noticed him—his eyes glassy and faraway with a gentle, incessant, and annoying humming emanating from him. It was the moment teachers since time immemorial have lived for: gotcha, you day-dreaming youth, you.

The teacher called on Tommy, demanding him to repeat something she had just said. Of course, Tommy could do no such thing. When his teacher demanded to know why he could not answer, Tommy responded honestly—he had been listening to the music in his head. Exasperated with the answer his teacher instructed Tommy to stand by his desk, then, and sing to the class what he had been hearing.

And so, he did. First, he sang the viola part he was hearing to the startled teacher, second, he sang for her the cello part, and finally the percussion.

The teacher promptly sent him to the school psychologist.[9] Bell would go on to compose some of the biggest smash hits of the 1970s, though it was clearly through no fault of his first-grade teacher.

Even after all of his life's success, Bell recalled "the painfully embarrassing first-grade lesson about subjecting himself to the ridicule of others. 'What a jackass I was,' he lamented. 'Too stupid to keep my mouth shut!'"[10] The extraordinary tunes playing inside Thom Bell's head, shared so beautifully with the world in songs recorded by the Spinners, the DelFonics, The Stylistics, Daryl Hall and John Oates, Elton John, and more, should have been a revelation to the class and a moment of triumph. Instead, Bell recalls it with shame. The faith of a teacher can make all the difference—an important reason we must stay vigilant against becoming cynics and abandoning hope in our profession. There is too much at stake for us to give in.

New teachers are often intuitively aware of this power and responsibility, which is why walking into your own classroom for the first time is both the most exhilarating and the most terrifying experience imaginable. As young teachers walk into their classroom and glance at the awe-inspiring, all-powerful seat of authority that is now theirs, they can feel overwhelming. They have spent decades on the other side of that desk, struggling to please and to pass and to avoid undue or unwanted attention, and now they will sit on the side with the prestige—the side with the power.

It is a moment in which the world's natural order seems to alter just a bit. There may also be the faces of former teachers smilingly, knowingly dancing through their heads. The teacher hit in the back of the head with the spitball in sixth grade. The teacher whose observation was ruined by tougher than usual questioning. The teacher whose legendary patience was tried by the giggles and the note passing. Yes, the young teacher may see those faces and dreadfully wonder if it is indeed true that "what comes around goes around."

But more than all that a young teacher walks into his or her classroom for the first time with a heart full of hope and a head full of ideas. Independence from those education program professors has finally been achieved. They no longer have to write their lesson plans in a certain format or develop lessons that please everyone but himself or herself. The portfolio is now neatly tucked away in an attic. The classroom's blank walls will soon be covered with symbols of their own personality and dreams. These teachers are often virtually walking on air with the thoughts of all the good they will do and the lives they will change.

In the weeks prior to showing up for work they have rented *Dead Poet's Society* and *Mr. Holland's Opus* and cried wistfully in their popcorn. That kind of near-euphoric idealism is difficult to sustain, however, and the slight but relentless chipping away of those hopes and dreams begins long before the first student even enters the class. In order to remain those pilgrims to the horizon, new teachers must protect themselves from the unprofessionalism and the cynicism that they will surely face once they are in a classroom. New teachers must prioritize and promote hope—in their students, the community, and the future, as well as combat any and all efforts to diminish their idealism or inhibit their spirit.

There is a process that begins immediately with new faculty that is something akin to a recruitment campaign. It begins the moment veteran faculty members begin to share their "wisdom" with their young counterparts—wisdom that too often is a mere euphemism for cynicism. This is not to say, of course, that they are not veteran faculty members who actually do have wisdom to impart, but it is often difficult for a young teacher to know whom to trust and whom to cast to the wind.

Faculties are often divided into "camps": there are the traditionalists versus the progressives (also known as the "fogies" versus the "permissives"); the stalwart union members versus those who believe the union is a communist front; and those who like the administration and those who want to undermine the administration at any and all opportunities also seek new blood.

As the young teacher sits in his or her classroom dreaming of how the students will learn and become great thinkers, these camps send their representatives to them and begin trying to pull the new guy into their sphere of influence. This can be dizzying, confusing, and disheartening for a young and an idealistic educator.

"Be careful of Mr. Haney," Mrs. Jones tells you, "He's an incorrigible gossip."

"Watch your back with Mrs. Jones," Mr. Haney tells you the next day, "She runs to the director with everything you say."

"You may have a tough time with some of your kids this year," Mrs. Smith tells you conspiratorially in the lounge one afternoon. "They had Mr. Love last year for social studies and he never does anything but read the book to them. Good luck."

"Mrs. Smith got her Master's degree in education last May," Mr. Love tells you one afternoon in the parking lot, "and now the old battle ax wants to tell everyone how to do their job. She's become a total know-it-all."

It goes without saying that this kind of childish backbiting is anything but helpful and is anything but professional. But it is also terribly destructive in the way it can color a young teacher's attitude toward her new job. When Woodrow Wilson was asked why he left higher education to run for public office, he is said to have replied it was because he wanted to get *out* of politics. Teacher training programs should not allow young teachers to leave their campus without understanding the kind of pettiness that they may encounter and without trying to provide them with some tools for coping with this maneuvering.

The effort to force a new teacher to take sides in long-simmering personal or ideological battles is harmful to the new teacher's morale (as it is to the morale of the school as a whole in the long run), but there is a more insidious sharing of "insider information" that also occurs before the school year begins—the labeling of students in order to "help" new teachers succeed.

Some Christian denominations believe that there is a text in the afterlife known as the "Book of Life" in which all of one's sins are recorded to be answered for on Judgment Day. If this is true, I imagine the book may be based on the record kept of every student's missteps by some former teachers. These teachers feel the need to take a walk across the hall or across campus to fill the head of the current teacher about how rotten certain students are or will be.

Any student can easily tell you that a reputation once developed among a school's faculty is like the mark of Cain. We might as well adopt Hawthorne's method and force these students to wear shirts with a large red "T" emblazoned on the front signifying Trouble. Often it is the previous year's teacher who stops by one afternoon to give an earful about the students you have inherited.

They come in, sit in one of the student's chairs, and glance knowingly and darkly at the roster sheet. They then proceed to go down the list—one by one—and explain who are the good students, who are the bad students, who's ADD, whose mother is a complainer, who writes poorly, who doesn't do any homework and who does, who will be a constant check mark on the absentee list, and on and on. Clearly a student's former teacher or teachers can be a valuable asset for a young teacher (or a struggling veteran one for that matter).

But for that to be the case, the former teacher must approach the situation from a strong desire to see each child succeed. Sadly, this is not always the case. Too often it is approached from a malicious perspective, the former teacher seems almost giddy at the prospect that someone else now has to deal with these students. In such a case, it seems no wonder that he or she struggled to make positive connections with any student at all.

One sixth-grade teacher tells the following story:

> One of the students [a coworker] labeled for me was a young man who the year before had gotten into terrible trouble for stealing a golf cart that was

property of the school and then driving it around campus, tearing up the lawns. He had pulled this off for weeks without getting caught. Once he was caught, he seemed anything but contrite at what had happened; in fact, I was told he seemed deeply amused at the trouble and consternation he had caused.

By the time his former teacher was finished talking about him, I was convinced that I needed to invest in body armor before trying to teach this modern Sundance Kid. Nothing could have been further from the truth. Whether this young man had learned a lesson from being caught or simply matured over the summer I cannot say; but what I can say is that he was one of the best students in my class that year. In fact, he was one of the best students I have ever taught. Had I based my actions and attitudes towards him on his reputation, it would no doubt have been a far different experience for us both.

Sometimes it is a parent or parents who try to give a new teacher a "head's up" about any number of things—from the students to the other parents to the faculty and administration. These situations are especially dicey, because a new teacher has no desire to start off on the wrong foot with a parent. While not bound by the same professional ethics as teachers, these parents inevitably do more harm than good. Let me be clear: I believe strongly that every child should be afforded the chance to begin each school year with a clean slate.

Last year's trouble with algebra or talkativeness or even contempt for authority should not be carried over. Labeling these students in the minds of a teacher before the student has the chance to prove himself or herself does a terrible injustice to that student. The possibility of a self-fulfilling prophecy is too powerful to be ignored in these situations. If students turn out to be absolute demons, so be it. But this should be a judgment based on *this year's* actions, not last year's or the last decades.

This sort of labeling gives the impression that some educators do not believe in the possibility that one may change over time and that one may mature or grow physically, spiritually, and cognitively. If an educator indeed feels this way, then he or she should retire immediately before afforded the chance to do any damage to a young life. At the very least, they should have the good sense to keep their cynicism to themselves.

On December 23, 1857, a haggard-looking man shifted on the balls of his feet inside the warmth of the little pawnshop. His countenance was a tragic mix of embarrassment and humiliation. It was Christmas season and he had a pregnant wife and three children at home. The economic collapse of 1857 had devastated the nation, and with his farm an utter loss, he was reduced to selling firewood on the streets of Saint Louis just to make ends meet.

Faced with no good options, he dejectedly removed his gold watch and chain from his trousers pocket and, negotiating as best as he could for a desperate man in a desperate hour, pawned the items for money he could use to purchase holiday presents for his family. As he departed the shop and stepped out into the bustling holiday traffic, there was nothing to indicate what lay store for the down-on-his-luck ne'er do well would-be farmer.

Just over a decade after this personal nadir, Ulysses S. Grant was an American war hero and legend and the newly inaugurated president of the United States. Grant's transformation from bum to world leader is just one powerful reminder that we are not static beings—we are ever changing and developing. Educational philosophy and educators must reflect this understanding of *becoming* as a central tenet of the profession.

Alfred North Whitehead's process theory (discussed further in chapter 6) is desperately important for teachers in this regard. "Process," Malcolm D. Evans writes, "refers to becoming and being resulting from an inheritance of the past and an aim for the future. Every living thing and some supposedly inanimate objects reflect this. We are becoming something different at every moment."[11] Whitehead said:

> It took a long while, centuries in fact, for philosophers to get beyond the idea of static matter. Certain substances, like water or fire, could be seen to be changing rapidly; others, like rock, looked immutable. We know now that a piece of granite is a raging mass of activity, that it is changing at a terrific rate; but until we did know it, a rock seemed to possess little or no life, though it looked immensely permanent. . . . Our human bodies change from day to day; certain external appearances of them are the same, but change is constant and sometimes visible. The constellations do not appear to change at all, though we know that they do. . . . Change is constant, whether we measure it by minutes or millennia; we ourselves are part of it.[12]

Every student must be allowed the opportunity to grow, to show their development, and, ultimately, to succeed.

To do this, teachers must trash labels and boxes and anything that stands as an obstacle to the fresh start every student deserves every single day of their school career. Perrone notes the need for this disposition as well, writing that teachers need to possess "a general interest in human growth and development."[13] There is nearly nothing that combats cynicism as much as simply admitting the possibility for, and the hope of, change.

There is no greater symbol of the threat of cynicism to new teachers than the teacher's lounge, which is often a forum for the complaints and frustrations of teachers and staff. The conversations in a teacher's lounge hold the power to demolish the idealism and the hopes of a new educator. To hear the discussions in a teacher's lounge can easily cause one to assume that there is nothing but failure and misery in a school.

It needs to be said here that there is nothing inherently wrong with teachers gathering together to share their concerns and to seek guidance in dealing with these problems—whether real or perceived. That is the entire point of collegial relationships; we learn from those who have more experience or more expertise (natural or gained) in a certain topic or topics. Knowing that experience is the greatest educator, we lean on those who have faced a particular situation and borrow what they did right and discard that which did not succeed.

The problem with the conversations in many teachers' lounges is that they are not for the purpose of seeking solutions, but rather the airing of "dirty laundry," or just simple complaining. When some students at Valparaiso University complained to Senator Robert F. Kennedy in 1968 that the federal government wasn't doing enough for the poor, Kennedy turned the complaint back on the privileged students.

"Well, you tell me something now," he demanded.

> How many of you spent time over the summer, or on vacations, working in a black ghetto, or in eastern Kentucky, or on Indian reservations? Instead of asking what the federal government is doing about starving children, I say, what is your responsibility? What are you going to do about it? I think you people should organize yourselves right here and try to do something about it.[14]

That should be our attitude toward conversations about problems—what are our proposed solutions? Without an eye toward solutions or objectives, these discussions are petty and bitter. This problem is not confined to education. I imagine the conversation during lunch break at a construction site sound eerily similar to those in the teacher's lounge. But there is an important difference. As educators we are constructing minds, not buildings, and we have the power to do far more damage when we sit around castigating aspects of our school or our students.

If we truly believe that education is a moral endeavor, then we owe it to our students and, indeed our colleagues and ourselves, to refrain from the very human instinct to decry and emphasize the negative. These conversations, innocent perhaps in their intent, are insidious in their outcomes and manifestations. The discussions revolve around three major topics: the administration, the parents, and the students themselves. In each case the darkness of tone and the frustrated anger in the words are enough to scare any new teacher back to school for a new degree and career path.

The Administration

Complaining about THE BOSS is as natural, it seems, as breathing. In America, especially in the workplace, we are all populists. We don't like authority, particularly when it is lorded over our heads. There is a stubborn strain of resistance seemingly built into the American character. This hardheadedness goes way back in American history. In March 1676, as King Philip raged war across New England, the town of Rehoboth was attacked by as many as 1,500 Indian allies of the Pokanoket leader.

In spite of the overwhelming odds only one Pilgrim resident was killed that day

> a man who believed that as long as he continued to read the Bible, no harm would come to him. Refusing to abandon his home, he was found shot to death in his chair—the Bible still in his hands.[15]

Don't tread on me or tell me what to do. In education it can be especially troubling, because teaching is such an intensely intimate and personal style-driven occupation. None of us would want someone to critique the way we pray, and we don't care for it when our teaching is critiqued, either.

But that is the very function of an administrator to guide and develop our teaching, whether we like it or not. THE BOSS comes in and observes our classes, he or she is the one called when parents are upset, and he or she is the one forced to correct the teacher when we step out of line. None of that makes for easy friendships. There is also the attitude of many teachers that an administrator is someone who could not cut it in the classroom. All of this combines for what can easily be a tense standoff between the teachers and the administrators.

This tension manifests itself in the lounge where, with the door closed tightly, the teachers lash out. There is always one teacher who has perfected a near-perfect impression of THE BOSS and will happily perform it at the drop of a hat. There may be veteran teachers who were already in their own classroom when THE BOSS was first learning about Bloom's taxonomy in college. Maybe THE BOSS is relatively new to the school and has the temerity to propose new ways of doing things.

Whatever the reasons, a new teacher should not be subjected to the constant belittling of the administration due to the effect this is likely to have on his or her opinion of THE BOSS (which may align with the others' frustrations, but should be learned objectively and not from second-hand complaining) and his or her job. Moreover, the recruitment process described earlier continues on in the lounge.

A new teacher is not likely to feel comfortable or confident enough to disagree with the veterans and their assessments of the administration, and since those who are silent are thought to consent, the opinions of the others may be ascribed to the young teacher. Finally, a young teacher is in a dangerous position in these conversations. Veteran educators may be established well enough to opine on the shortcomings of the administration with little fear of reprisal, but the new teacher is not. It is a distinctly bad idea to begin your career faced with an acrimonious relationship with THE BOSS.

The Parents

The second group that comes in for bashing in the teacher's lounge is parents. It is all too easy for teachers and parents to develop an adversarial relationship. Parents pay the taxes that pay a teacher's salary, and entrust their children to a teacher's care and influence. There is no greater responsibility than to care for someone's child, and with this responsibility comes the occasional misunderstanding. It is entirely understandable for educators to feel micromanaged and second-guessed when parents, in groups or as individuals, call to complain or send tart notes.

It is not understandable, however, indeed it is inexcusable, for teachers to vent this frustration in the teacher's lounge in some of the language that is often heard. In addition to the compassion and empathy educators must have for our students, we must also exhibit these same traits toward their parents. We cannot fathom, no matter how full of empathy we fancy ourselves, the depth of love, devotion, and concern a parent has for their child.

Becoming a parent changes a person; it makes one just a little insane. Although parents may be overbearing and domineering, we owe them the same compassion we show to our students. We have no business sitting in the lounge and practicing pop psychology in front of our colleagues, diagnosing a mother or father's neuroses and mocking them.

One of the constant complaints I hear from teachers (and have made myself) is that we are not treated as professionals. If we truly desire to be seen as professionals, *then the first step is to begin acting like professionals*. Denigrating the parents of our students for any reason is simply not a part of professionalism. If a parent crosses the line, becoming abusive or derogatory in a conference or during a conversation, that is not the fodder for the lounge. The teacher in question should take such an issue immediately to the administration. That is where such an issue belongs. Not in the lounge.

The Students

It should not even need to be written that we do not sit around mocking or deploring our students in the lounge. But it does. The problem here is not merely that such a behavior is not designed to seek solutions or assistance, but it is that such conversations are unethical and immoral. A teacher going into the lounge and saying, "I am having trouble getting through to Johnny, do you have any suggestions?" is a positive interaction. "Johnny is a lazy kid" is not. The conversations about students that take place in the teacher's lounge frequently serve only to perpetuate the labeling of students.

It is not always negative, of course. It may be a conversation about what a hard worker Lisa is or how bright Sam is. But if we go to the lounge to label some bright, we are likely to label others, in contrast, as not as bright, and that is dangerous. Many of the conversations occurring in the lounge about students are not only unprofessional but also unethical. A young teacher relying on the opinion of the pseudo-sages in the lounge will take the chance of missing the opportunity to take kids on their own terms and meet them with the blank slate mentioned earlier.

The mere chance that any of the harmful and hateful things said about some students in the lounge might escape into the school and, more disastrously, into the ears of the student being "discussed" is one not worth taking. A teacher should say nothing in the lounge to her peers that she would not or has not also said to a student's parents. That must be our rule of thumb. This rule does not exclude the possibility of seeking counsel, but rids us of the possibility that we will merely be gossiping or putting down our students.

In some ways, the teacher's lounges of today have improved over the ones when I was a kid. I can recall teachers leaving the lounge at my elementary school and the cigarette smoke billowing out behind them as if we were all in a Cheech and Chong movie. But the substantive issues remain. Many preservice teachers are afraid of avoiding the lounge because they do not want to be labeled aloof or snobbish.

This is a valid concern, but my advice remains the same: stay away. If you become labeled then so be it. There are worse things, among them being an educator who sits around talking in unprofessional and unhelpful ways about the administration, parents, teachers, or even fellow teachers. Although as a new teacher you want to remain above the fray as much as possible, you should not interpret this to mean that you must compromise your ideals or principles.

When a colleague comes to your room to trash a student or a group of students, there is nothing wrong in telling that colleague: "Thanks for trying to help, I appreciate it, but I really don't want to hear that stuff. I would rather approach my new class with no preconceptions and see how it goes." That is polite and professional and sets your peer straight quickly. He or she may shrug, call you naïve and laugh, but so be it. You will have done your students a favor and made the likelihood of your own success greater.

That same statement may also be applied to parents eager to share their information. There may be some concern that staying "above the fray" will make you a loner and an outcast on the faculty. That is a possibility, and one every teacher should be willing to accept. We do not become teachers so that we may befriend other teachers, but so that we might make a difference. Moreover, not every teacher is a gossip, or a cynic. The good teachers tend to find each other and support each other in ways that are more conducive to success.

Idealism remains the lifeblood of a teacher, a sustaining and nurturing force that makes the challenges surmountable and the dark days survivable. A creeping and insidious cynicism is a malignancy to an educator. Cynicism denies hope, and hope is the very essence of education. We might well hope that education could become how Reinhold Niebuhr defined religion as "a citadel of hope, which is built on the edge of despair."[16] New teachers face enough challenges without having to guard against your own colleagues, and it must be noted that many if not most of your fellow teachers will inspire, challenge, and support you.

But it is the height of naivete not to acknowledge the efforts of other educators to drag you down to their level. Indeed, you will confront incompetent administrators, disrespectful parents, and deeply challenging students. None of that is false or shocking. Finding those coworkers who help us rise above, rather than wallow in the muck, is vital to a long and successful career.

In the early fall of 2001, a hungry, young, upstart politician had lunch with a Washington, D.C., media consultant. The potential candidate was batting .500 in his quest for office, having won a state legislative seat before being summarily trounced after his ego outpaced his sense and he attempted to primary an entrenched veteran politician. Now he wanted back in the game and had his eyes on a US Senate seat. The media advisor, however, had a dose of cold reality for the young man.

> "Hell of a thing," he said, shaking his head. "Really bad luck. You can't change your name, of course. Voters are suspicious of that kind of thing. Maybe if you were at the start of your career, you know, you could use a nickname or something. But now . . ." His voice trailed off and he shrugged apologetically before signaling the waiter to bring us the check.[17]

Earlier in the lunch, the advisor reminded the aspiring senator that "the political dynamics have changed" before nodding to the newspaper on the table in front of them with Osama bin Laden's photograph splashed across the front page.[18]

With the Twin Towers still smoldering, there was simply no way a man named Barack Hussein Obama had any shot at getting elected. None. Yet we know how this story ends; Obama became a successful two-term president and, at the time of this writing, remains the most popular and respected political figure on earth. Running on a platform of hope and change he ignited the dreams of a generation. He writes that hope represents "the best of the America spirit," and described it as "the audacity to believe despite all the evidence to the contrary."[19] This crystallizes the attitude a teacher must carry. Our students deserve our hope. Remain a pilgrim to the horizon for and with your students. Confront and defeat cynicism.

Notes

1. Zora Neale Hurston, *Dust Tracks on a Road* (New York: Harper Perennial, 1942), p. 1.

2. Valerie Boyd, *Wrapped In Rainbows: The Life of Zora Neale Hurston* (New York: Scribner, 2003), p. 19.

3. Hurston, *Dust Tracks on a Road*, p. 25.

4. Hurston, *Dust Tracks on a Road*, p. 34.

5. Hurston, *Dust Tracks on a Road*, p. 13.

6. Hurston, *Dust Tracks on a Road*, p. 13.

7. Hurston, *Dust Tracks on a Road*, p. 107.

8. Hurston, *Dust Tracks on a Road*, p. 107.

9. John A. Jackson, *A House on Fire: The Rise and Fall of Philadelphia Soul* (London: Oxford University Press, 2004), location 200 Kindle edition.

10. Jackson, *A House on Fire*, location 208 Kindle edition.

11. Malcolm D. Evans, *Whitehead and Philosophy of Education: The Seamless Coat of Learning* (Amsterdam: Rodopi, 1998), p. 61.

12. Lucien Price, *Dialogues of Alfred North Whitehead* (Boston, MA: Nonpareil Book, 1954), pp. 209–210.

13. Vito Perrone, *Lessons for New Teachers* (Boston, MA: McGraw Hill, 2000), p. 10.

14. Thurston Clarke, *The Last Campaign: Robert F. Kennedy and 82 Days that Inspired America* (New York: Henry Holt, 2008), p. 189.

15. Nathaniel Philbrick, *Mayflower: A Story of Courage, Community, and War* (New York: Viking, 2006), p. 300.

16. Reinhold Niebuhr, *Moral Man and Immoral Society; A Study in Ethics and Politics* (Louisville, KY: Westminster John Knox Press, 1932), p. 62.

17. Barack Obama, *The Audacity of Hope* (New York: Three Rivers Press, 2006), p. 3.
18. Obama, *The Audacity of Hope*, p. 3.
19. Obama, *The Audacity of Hope*, p. 356.

CHAPTER 3

Rowing to Galveston

Remember when the word "liberal" was not an expletive in American political life? If you're under thirty years of age, the chance is that you do not. Both the idea and the ideal of *liberal* were done no favors—some might argue were irreparably harmed—by the indelible image of Massachusetts governor and Democratic presidential nominee Michael Dukakis tooling around in a tank with his bulbous noggin stuffed tightly (and by all appearances uncomfortably) in his green helmet.

The year was 1988, and Dukakis was running against then Vice President George H.W. Bush for the White House. In an attempt to portray himself as tough on defense and a man who understood the military, someone in the campaign decided to send the governor around, in front of the cameras, in that tank. Unfortunately for his presidential aspirations, Dukakis looked like an idiot. He resembled Snoopy more than Sherman. The unforgettable image was pure gold for the late-night comedians (and almost everyone else with even a semblance of a sense of humor) and made Dukakis seem like a far-left softie.

The photo-op was a disaster. The problem was not that Dukakis was less than photogenic, although that case could be made. The problem was that long before the photo-op was even dreamed up Dukakis had allowed himself to be defined by *others*, in this case his political opponents. Tooling around in that tank was a reaction to someone else's idea of who Dukakis was and what a liberal was; there is a lesson here for teachers.

A different but closely related lesson might be drawn from the example of the Smothers Brothers, Tom and Dick, during their groundbreaking and now-legendary variety show and its battles with CBS network censors. Described as "introducing and encouraging new talent, pushing the boundaries of network television, and reflecting the youth movement and embracing its antiwar stance and anti-administration politics," *The Smothers Brothers Comedy Hour* aired from 1967 to 1969 and was controversial almost from the start.[1]

Labeled by a thoroughly petrified establishment as subversive, the brothers and their writers decided to have some fun at the expense of the censors by making the most of the label. Quietly, the show's creative talent—"dancers, singers, even the camera operators and costumers"—were instructed to explode in uproarious laughter whenever they heard the phrase "rowing to Galveston."[2]

Part Lewis Carroll, part George Orwell, the phrase was a meaningless concoction of the writers and, especially, Tommy Smothers and it worked to perfection, driving the network censors to distraction as they scurried and scrambled to discover the phrase's origin and meaning. The paranoid panicking delighted Tommy Smothers, though it likely failed to endear him to his bosses at CBS.

The censors became "unhinged by the 'dirty laughter' it invariably elicited from the cast and crew," the Brothers' biographer noted.[3] The phrase was everywhere—*rowing to Galveston*—sometimes actually in the script and other times tossed out as an ad-lib, and the suits were convinced the words, like the talismanic lyrics to "Louie Louie" before, was bound to lead America's youth straight to hell.

Though it had no meaning at all, the phrase was always excised from the show. Always. When Tommy Smothers once demanded to know why, a CBS executive sputtered, "You *know* why!"[4] What good was it being labeled subversive, the brothers seemed to ask, if you weren't going to subvert? The Smothers Brothers took their label and ran with it, to hilarious if self-defeating results (the show was canceled after only three seasons).

One of the first teaching jobs I had was at a private middle school—a very posh private middle school. The culture of the school was practically antebellum; it was deeply conservative and determined to keep the students safe from controversy or modernity. At the time I was hired, I had three earrings in my left ear, two in my right, hair down between my shoulder blades, and a fair assortment of tattoos. Needless to say, I did not look like what the students or the parents had come to expect in a teacher at this school. The result was that many of the parents began to define me, as did some members of the faculty and the administration, according to their own beliefs and fears.

At first, this was merely annoying to me, but I soon found myself unable to effectively do my job because of the labels some had placed on me. These labels were often amusing: unreformed hippie, radical liberal, Woodstock wannabe, and of course communist. But others, such as bad influence, dangerous influence, and someone of questionable character, were not at all amusing, because they directly affected my ability to teach my students. I quickly discovered that when a teacher begins to parse words and filter his curriculum through a prism of fear, that teacher can no longer do his job well, and it is the students who suffer.

My Dukakis moment came early in my career with the *Great El Norte Massacre*. My sixth-grade social studies class was studying Mexico, and one of my colleagues suggested that I show them the film *El Norte*. This colleague told me that it was a powerful film, and that they had shown it during this particular unit the previous three years. I took the advice and went to Blockbuster to rent the film.

My first surprise came when I saw that the film was rated R. I was pretty sure it was bad form to show a film with this rating to sixth graders, but I was also new to this school, and decided it was better to just go along with the tradition of showing it during the study of Mexico. After all, I had been told it was an "eye-opening" look at the plight of immigrants to the United States.

I showed the film to my first two periods, and I was stunned at what I saw. There was a scene which showed a man's severed head. There were more expletives—all in subtitles—than I usually spew at the referees during a Tarheels basketball game. The "F" bomb was dropped with the frequency of the London Blitz, as were other profanities of equal color. At the end of the second period, I caught the colleague (who was also my immediate supervisor) in the hall.

"Okay," I said, "you've got to tell me what I'm doing wrong. They're not walking out of my class talking about the plight of immigrants. They're all walking out of my class laughing at the foul-mouthed Mexican truck driver."

He looked at me incredulously.

"What foul-mouthed Mexican truck driver?" he asked.

It was at that moment that my entire career flashed before my eyes. "What foul-mouthed Mexican truck driver" was not the anticipated or hoped for response. Since third period was my planning period, my colleague and I went into my room and I showed him the film. He turned a ghastly white. Some of the scenes he recognized as ones he had shown, but the most questionable and offensive scenes he had never seen before.

It only took a little investigating to learn that the previous social studies teacher had indeed rented *El Norte*, but he had brought it to the school's library and, using the dual-deck VCR, edited the film so that there were no scenes of beheaded men and there was no foul-mouthed Mexican truck driver. Somehow that had happened without my boss ever learning about it.

When I arrived at work the next morning, there was line of parents stretching outside my director's office demanding that *my* severed head be placed atop the flag pole. That wasn't so bad, since the school offered an excellent benefits package—but they were also demanding that I be fired before the beheading. Luckily, I wasn't fired. But I did have to send home a humiliating letter stating that I was young, deeply sorry, and genuflecting in all sorts of directions.

Some parents accepted the apology, but a small group felt that they now had the proof that they needed to prove that a man with earrings and long hair had no business teaching their children. I spent the remainder of the year trying to instill passion in my students for social studies, but also watching my back and trying to convince the cabal of angry parents that I was not a moral reprobate.

This anecdote illustrates a vital lesson: teachers must learn to define *themselves* before others apply their own stereotypes or ignorance to them. Teachers must learn the art of *framing*—their profession, their pedagogy, and their passion—in order to take command of the conversation surrounding our profession. "Frames," George Lakoff writes, "are the mental structures that allow human beings to understand reality—and sometimes to create what we take to be reality."[5]

He further explains, "Frames facilitate our most basic interactions with the world—they structure our ideas and concepts, they shape the way we reason, and they even impact how we perceive and how we act."[6] It is time for teachers to frame teaching, not politicians, not administrators, not parents, but *Teachers*. There is no trick to this, it is a matter of communication of reaching out to the parents and the school community before you get tagged with a label of someone else's choosing.

This kind of communication is invaluable for the teacher, because it serves to introduce her to the community in a personal, one-on-one way, and allows the new teacher to frame his or her approach and style and personality. Such communication allows the teacher to define himself in the eyes of the school community as much as is possible.

It is worth exploring at this point how teachers *are* perceived in America today. If a recent survey is to be believed, well over half of Americans rate public schools C grade (54 percent).[7] There is, in fact, widespread agreement that American schools are embarrassingly mediocre, with nearly identical percentages of parents (53 percent), teachers (54 percent), Republicans (53 percent), and Democrats (55 percent) grading American schools with grade

C.[8] Importantly, however, nearly a third of parents (30 percent) would evaluate *their* child's teacher as "excellent."[9]

In fact, 63 percent of the parents rated *their* child's teacher as "excellent" or "good," with only 14 percent rated their child's teacher as "unsatisfactory."[10] In the spring of 2018, a remarkable 62 percent of Americans surveyed believed that teachers are underpaid, with a paltry 9 percent thinking teachers make too much money.[11] In December 2018, a Gallup poll found that 60 percent of Americans believed high-school teachers had high or very high "honesty and ethical standards."[12] The view of teachers and education among young Americans is equally positive.

Majorities of millennials across racial groups view their own educational experience as positive, with 75 percent of Asian Americans, 65 percent of whites, 56 percent of African Americans, and 59 percent of Latinx millennials giving their education an "A" or "B" grade.[13] This demographic also agrees on the three most important ways to improve schools, and they include increasing both school funding and teacher's pay.[14] This group mirrors their parents in seeing teachers as both underpaid and undervalued. More concerningly, though, millennials also mirror their parents in seeing the larger school system as failing, "giving much lower grades to the nation's public schools" than to their own school.[15]

Parents and students alike rate their own schools and experiences highly yet are convinced that "America's schools" are disastrous failures. That is because the enemies of America's public schools and public school system have relentlessly framed American schools and teachers as failing since at least the 1980s. Yes, I love my local school and my child's teacher, but *America's schools* are a terrible, terrible failure, and a national disgrace.

This Big Lie has been perpetuated across the political spectrum, with Democrats and Republicans alike taking incessant potshots at educators. Legislatures eviscerate education and social program budgets and then conveniently blame teachers when hungry children fail to make adequate progress as defined by (typically) white men who have never stood in a classroom. These unrelenting pressures and stress, the lack of sufficient pay, and the near-constant disrespect from policy makers have combined to devastating effect on how teachers view ourselves and our jobs.

The emerging crisis became apparent in 2013, in the much-publicized MetLife Teacher Survey. The results revealed that teacher's satisfaction with their job had declined a stunning 23 percent between 2008 and 2012 and stood at its lowest level in a quarter century.[16] Fifty-one percent of the teachers told researchers they felt "under great stress several days a week."[17] Fifty-six percent of the teachers in 2012 reported that their school had faced budget cuts in the previous twelve months, and half of the teachers felt managing their school budget was "very challenging."[18]

These challenges had only deepened in 2019, and the results were the same. That year's Phi Delta Kappa Poll found that "half of public school teachers nationally have seriously considered leaving the profession in the past few years—and majorities . . . say that given the opportunity, they'd vote to strike."[19]

Incredibly, 2019 was the *eighteenth consecutive year* that "Americans continue[d] to express their concern about the lack of financial support for the public schools, naming this as the biggest problem facing their local schools," with 60 percent responding that schools were provided "too little money."[20] Sixty percent of teachers in 2019 felt "they're unfairly paid," and, most tragically of all, 55 percent of teachers "would not want their child to follow them into the profession."[21] Whipped by the political winds and battered by three decades of demonization, teachers are exhausted.

To counter the ubiquitous negative framing, teachers must step up, take back our narrative, and move perception closer to reality. One challenge in achieving this reframing, of course, is that the public has applied their own frames to the profession over the years, so we are not beginning from a blank slate. Possibly, the first frame of the teacher was the image of an Ichabod Crane-type character; a lone male, bookish, ill-tempered, and sick; Shakespearean sonnets in one hand, a whip in the other. The influence of Horace Mann and Catherine Beecher transformed this frame as female teachers replaced male. This era framed teachers as "non-college-educated, unmarried, low-paid mother substitutes."[22]

That frame remains reality for a large degree of Americans. For others, there is a more insidious and frightening frame—educators as part of a cabal of "atheists, agnostics, and other secular humanists" who have "built up their forces and even increased their assault upon all our Christian institutions, and . . . been enormously successful in taking over the 'public square.'"[23]

This description comes from an influential 1996 evangelical text *The Gates of Hell Shall Not Prevail: The Attack on Christianity and What You Need to Know to Combat It* by Dr. D. James Kennedy, a Florida pastor and a personality. "Public education," he concludes, "now belong[s] to them."[24] In this frame, teachers are demonized as insufficiently patriotic and/or religious and are held out as threats to traditional order.

In our democratic republic, we must not hesitate to frame our profession in bold and transcendent terms. We must not fail to remind our communities of what we are—the frontline defense for equality, democratic principles, and, indeed, freedom. A high-quality, vibrant, respected public school system is the surest guarantor of the promises and potential of America and her people.

This view is reflected in the way South Korea defines teachers—*frames* teachers—as "nation builders."[25] We must reframe the idea of *Teacher* to one of professionalism; intellectually capable and curious; voracious readers; men and women of scholarship possessed of strong convictions and ideals but open to constant reflection and reinvention; community leaders; and tireless, relentless advocates for our students and all children.

The first step in this vital process is both simple and profound and is best described by the words of Saint Francis: preach the Gospel and, if necessary, use words. Do we want to be viewed as all those things listed above? *Then we must be those things.* No shortcuts, no excuses. *Esse quam videri*; to be rather than to seem. All else is pretense at best, hypocrisy at worst. To be perceived as voracious readers, we must read voraciously. Every day that we walk into our classroom we should carry with us whatever book we are reading at that moment—let our students see us devouring a book.

Do we wish to be known as scholars? One of the earliest definitions of that word comes from the Greek word *skholē*, which roughly translates to the knowledge gained in our leisure time. In other words, our time away from our students is at least partly spent in the search for new knowledge and information. To be seen as true advocates for our students, we must tirelessly advocate for them.

The great Carl Sagan reminds us that one of the oldest short essays in human history, written almost four thousand years ago by Sumer, "laments that the young are disastrously more ignorant than the generation immediately preceding."[26] Youth have been hearing for millennia how they fail to live up to the oft-only imagined heights of their ancestors. They need rather to be reminded constantly that the future is theirs. This is our calling.

Educators who are constantly engaged in reevaluating our curriculum, our methods, and our goals also aid the image of a teacher we are constructing. It is far too easy in the teaching profession to become complacent with our own methods and never to venture beyond our own comfort zones. Teachers rely heavily on textbooks or lesson plans formed decades ago with little questioning of their effectiveness. The idea seems to be that if a lesson worked once, it will work forever and ever. Of course, this is a ridiculous idea, as any good teacher will attest.

One can easily walk into a classroom with a plan that succeeds beautifully in first period and then bombs mercilessly in second period. Understanding this, it is hard to imagine why someone might think that a lesson plan written in 2002 would work in 2020, and yet this seems to be the attitude of too many in our profession. Each and every teacher should be involved in a constant process of questioning and reevaluating. We must take nothing for granted, and we must never assume that the methods and/or materials that worked in the past will continue to work *ad infinitum*.

The distinctive character of generations changing hands has been placed on hyper drive in our society—so that what works with students one year may not work the very next year, because students' lives are changing so quickly. If educators admit the frightening truth that students are a collection of distinct individuals rather than cattle, then we must always think of new and exciting ways to reach out to them.

Despite the phenomenal success of McDonalds throughout the world, the company is not still selling hamburgers with the same slogans and ad campaigns that worked in the 1950s. We may safely assume that education has not had the global impact as has McDonalds, so we may also assume that none of our pedagogical approaches deserve to be encased in amber and treated as sacrosanct.

As we seek to reframe both the perception and the reality of being a teacher, one of the first and most important things we must do is to share our passion for our vocation. Displaying this passion is something many teachers never do. One powerful reason that we often fail to show our passion to our students is because it makes us vulnerable. This is something we have been conditioned to avoid, in or out of the classroom. To let our passion show through means to admit that we are indeed the geeks they suspect us of being.

Yes, we watch the History Channel and often record documentaries to watch again and again. We are not sure we want anyone except our significant others to know this dreadful truth about us. But teaching without passion is like dancing without music. If we do not let our excitement for the subject matter and the learning process show through, how do we dare believe our students might care about what we tell them? *Passion is contagious.* It infects those who come into its presence because it is authentic and precisely because the passionate person so willingly becomes vulnerable.

Another key to reframing the perceptions of our vocation is learning to artfully communicate our vision of the job. There is an activity I do with my pre-service teachers called "defending your honor." This activity asks my students to write an essay detailing an answer to their future students when they are asked when they will ever use the information we are giving them, or why they need to know it in the first place. This is an important exercise that every new (and veteran) teacher should do frequently throughout the school year and in their career.

Too often students' questions of "why" are answered with cynical brevity—because I said so, or because it's on the test. These are not answers, nor are they even approaching the kind of respect we as educators owe to the young people and children in our care. Our students demanding to know a quantifiable benefit to their study reflects the society in which we live. Education for the sake of knowledge or personal enhancement is anachronistic in our culture; our students have been brought up to expect that we will ultimately provide them with "marketable skills" that will allow them to succeed in the corporate world.

This, in turn, will allow them to have the fancy house with the circle drive and the Rolex. Nothing else really matters. We should take the opportunity their question presents and make the most of it—this is our chance to shine. It is our chance to offer our students a glimpse of what a broad and challenging education can afford them. We must make the most of this chance. Answering the student with a critique of America's servile view of the role of education surely shows them that we have taken their question seriously.

We are always telling our students that we want them to become "thinkers." Of course, the very foundation of the personality of a true thinker, a true seeker, is one who questions. In a democracy, there are few habits of mind we can develop in children more essential than the willingness and ability to question—whether they question leaders, policies, or the dubious statements of "fact" that we are all bombarded with every day. As Chomsky writes, "Instead of indoctrinating students with democratic myths, schools should engage them in the practice of democracy" by honoring their questioning rather than shutting them down with blithe and vacuous answers.[27]

When our students ask us to defend our use of their childhood and adolescence, we must be ready to answer thoughtfully, effectively, and honestly. Such a stance also allows educators to constantly reevaluate our curriculum, its successes and failures, and its purpose. We should welcome the question "why do I need to know this" when asked by our students and we should be excited to answer it because this shows that we are willing to extend to our students that most basic human courtesy—we respect their views and honor their voice and concerns.

If thinkers across the vast continuum of history had never asked "why," we would be living in a far different and a less-enriched world. "Defending our honor" shows our students that we honor and respect their time, their views, and their voices. Answering our students also provides necessary evidence—for them as well as perhaps for us—that we are thinking practitioners and not the mindless automatons to which legislatures and too many schools of education have attempted to reduce us.

Along with our students we must communicate with parents and the larger community about who we are and what we do. Perrone writes, "We need more constructive relationships between teachers and parents, a more uplifting and more encouraging discourse."[28] Our students' parents and guardians need to be a part of the conversations in our classrooms and should be aware of what is happening within our curriculum.

Too often teachers only reach out to parents with the most mundane communications, such as scheduling changes, fundraisers, or field trips. This is insufficient; teachers should undertake a sustained line of communication with parents and guardians that invites them to be a part of their child's learning experience.

I urge my future teachers to send a letter home to parents on the very first day of school introducing themselves and telling the parents a little bit about themselves and what their children will be doing that year. In these letters, I think teachers can tell of their training (where they went to school, etc.), why they became a teacher, why they chose to teach their particular subject matter, and, if they are comfortable with it, a bit about their interests outside of school. This makes the teacher a person in the eyes of the parents and the students as well.

Teachers should make a habit out of sending notes home to parents that tell of the good things a child has done in class. One should never allow every note sent home to be negative. It is crucial to do as much of this communicating as early as possible. It is a mistake to have the first time you speak with a parent be when their child has broken a rule or forgotten an assignment.

These communications, this outreach, also desperately needs what Perrone calls "reciprocity."[29] This means when we share our stories, we should invite parents and guardians to do the same. Let parents and guardians know that they are welcome in our classes, and that we welcome their own stories and expertise. Rather than telling your students about veterans, if it is possible invite a veteran into your class. Again, Perrone reminds us "that making use of parent interests, skills, vocations, and avocations can enrich schools and classrooms and can build greater levels of parent-teacher and parent-school relationships."[30]

Knowing our parent constituency is also vital so that teachers avoid the pitfall of viewing parents in an adversarial or dismissive way. If we write off a parent or guardian as uncaring, unconcerned, uninvolved, or any of the myriad of snap judgments teachers often make, we lose the ability to connect with that guardian, and we also run the risk of being dreadfully wrong in our estimation. I have taught at Cherokee High School on the Qualla Boundary in North Carolina for seven years, and the relationship between Native Americans and institutions of "education" has been fraught throughout the history with abuse and cultural genocide.

Some parents avoid schools because they are traumatized, *not* because they fail to love their children. Many parents post smiling photos to social media of their child's big first day of kindergarten. Dennis Banks the Ojibwa Indian and founder of the American Indian Movement remembered the moment very very differently, referring to it as "the terrible day when the yellow bus arrived."[31] For many communities, particularly our most disadvantaged, there is a need to not only reframe the view of a teacher, but the very idea of the school needs to be redefined.

Banks continued,

> There is one dark day in the lives of all Indian children: the day when they are forcibly taken away from those who love and care for them, from those who speak their language. They are dragged, some screaming and weeping, others in silent terror, to a boarding school where they are remade into white kids.[32]

Such a history—not any lack of concern or care—may well keep parents away from the schoolhouse. Constant open lines of communication that share our vision for what an education can and should be can make us more sensitive and more effective in dealing with parents and guardians.

※

Marion Michael Morrison wanted to be a star. Although he was broad-shouldered, handsome, and a towering 6'4, Hollywood had a problem with Morrison. His name *Marion*, in particular, was found to be insufficiently "manly" for a leading man, and both his agent and a casting director urged Morrison to change it.[33] Morrison took the advice and transformed himself into John Wayne, uber-American and the very symbol of potent masculinity. Kimmel writes, "For much of the 1950s and for all of the 1960s and even into the 1970s, Wayne topped popularity polls as the American man that other American men most admired."[34]

Even with his new name and his physical stature, Wayne and Hollywood image makers left nothing to chance, with "sets . . . constructed so that he would appear too large for the tables and chairs at which he sat and . . . he was filmed from a slight upward angle to make him appear taller."[35] Unlike his contemporaries James Stewart, Henry Fonda, Clark Gable, and others, Wayne avoided service in World War II, and yet was viewed as the more masculine and even heroic than his Hollywood peers—at least to audiences. The framing of John Wayne was remarkably thorough and successful.

Two warnings from linguist George Lakoff will close our discussion of the vital need for teachers to take ownership of our image by framing our profession. First, he writes, "the truth alone will not set you free. Just speaking truth to power doesn't work. You need to frame the truths effectively from your perspective."[36] Second, and most importantly, he reminds his reader that "to be accepted, the truth must fit people's frames. If the facts do not fit a frame, the frame stays and the facts bounce off."[37]

Teachers are professionals, intellectuals, scholars, and leaders. We know this. Now we must frame the conversation so that Americans—from hostile legislature to worried moms and dads—will know this as well. We must do this for our own well-being as well as for the future generation of teachers who will follow.

Notes

1. David Bianculli, *Dangerously Funny: The Uncensored Story of the Smothers Brothers Comedy Hour* (New York: Touchstone, 2009), p. xi.

2. Bianculli, *Dangerously Funny*, p. 260.

3. Bianculli, *Dangerously Funny*, p. 260.

4. Bianculli, *Dangerously Funny*, p. 260.

5. George Lakoff, *Thinking Points: Communicating Our American Values and Vision* (New York: Farrar, Straus, and Giroux, 2006), p. 25.

6. Lakoff, *Thinking Points*, p. 25.

7. "Results from the 2017 Education Next Poll." Retrieved from https://www.educationnext.org/2017-ednext-poll-interactive/, January 1, 2020.

8. "Results from the 2017 Education Next Poll." Retrieved from https://www.educationnext.org/2017-ednext-poll-interactive/, January 1, 2020.

9. "Results from the 2017 Education Next Poll." Retrieved from https://www.educationnext.org/2017-ednext-poll-interactive/, January 1, 2020.

10. Results from the 2017 Education Next Poll." Retrieved from https://www.educationnext.org/2017-ednext-poll-interactive/, January 1, 2020.

11. "Americans Believe Teachers Are Underpaid." April 10, 2018. Retrieved from https://www.rasmussenreports.com/public_content/lifestyle/education/americans_believe_teachers_are_underpaid, January 1, 2020.

12. "Honesty/Ethics in Professions." Retrieved from https://news.gallup.com/poll/1654/honesty-ethics-professions.aspx, January 1, 2020.

13. Cathy J. Cohen, Matthew Fowler, Matthew D. Luttig, Vladimir E. Medenica, and Jon C. Rogowski, "Education in America: The Views of Millennials, A Summary of Key Findings from the First-of-its-kind Bimonthly Survey of Racially and Ethnically Diverse Young Adults," p. 4. Retrieved from http://genforwardsurvey

.com/assets/uploads/2017/09/GenForward-Education-Report_Final.pdf, January 1, 2020.

14. Cohen, Fowler, Luttig, Medenica, and Rogowski, "Education in America," p. 4.

15. Cohen, Fowler, Luttig, Medenica, and Rogowski, "Education in America," p. 4.

16. The MetLife Survey of the American Teacher: Challenges for School Leadership. February 2013, p. 6. Retrieved from https://www.metlife.com/content/dam/microsites/about/corporate-profile/MetLife-Teacher-Survey-2012.pdf, January 2, 2020.

17. The MetLife Survey, p. 6. Retrieved from https://www.metlife.com/content/dam/microsites/about/corporate-profile/MetLife-Teacher-Survey-2012.pdf, January 2, 2020.

18. The MetLife Survey, p. 5. Retrieved from https://www.metlife.com/content/dam/microsites/about/corporate-profile/MetLife-Teacher-Survey-2012.pdf, January 2, 2020.

19. 2019 PDK Poll of the Public's Attitudes toward the Public Schools. Retrieved from https://pdkpoll.org/results, January 2, 2020.

20. 2019 PDK Poll of the Public's Attitudes toward the Public Schools. Retrieved from https://pdkpoll.org/results, January 2, 2020.

21. 2019 PDK Poll of the Public's Attitudes toward the Public Schools. Retrieved from https://pdkpoll.org/results, January 2, 2020.

22. Dana Goldstein, *The Teachers Wars: A History of America's Most Embattled Profession* (New York: Anchor Books, 2014), p. 40.

23. Chris Hedges, *American Fascists: The Christian Right and the War on America* (New York: Free Press, 2009), pp. 58-59.

24. Hedges, *American Fascists*, p. 59.

25. Goldstein, *The Teachers Wars*, p. 4.

26. Carl Sagan, *The Demon-Haunted World: Science as a Candle in the Dark* (New York: Ballantine Books, 1996), Kindle location 234.

27. Noam Chomsky, *Chomsky on Miseducation*, Donaldo Macedo, Ed. (Lanham, MD: Rowman & Littlefield, 2000), p. 34.

28. Vito Perrone, *Lessons for New Teachers* (Boston, MA: McGraw Hill, 2000), p. 143.

29. Perrone, *Lessons for New Teachers*, p. 143.

30. Perrone, *Lessons for New Teachers*, p. 147.

31. Dennis Banks with Richard Erdoes, *Ojibwa Warrior: Dennis Banks and the Rise of the American Indian Movement* (Norman, OK: University of Oklahoma Press, 2004), p. 23.

32. Banks, *Ojibwa Warrior*, p. 24.

33. Michael Kimmel, *Manhood in America: A Cultural History* (New York: Oxford University Press, 2012), p. 182.

34. Kimmel, *Manhood in America*, p. 182.

35. Kimmel, *Manhood in America*, p. 182.

36. George Lakoff, *Don't Think of an Elephant: Know Your Values and Frame the Debate* (White River Junction, VT: Chelsea Green Publishing, 2004), p. 33.

37. Lakoff, *Don't Think of an Elephant*, p. 17.

CHAPTER 4

Standing on Desks

A healthy rebellious streak is as American as apple pie. We are, after all, a nation born in revolution with a founding document that acknowledges the peoples' creator-given right to overthrow the government whenever it fails to work for us. In popular culture, teachers are frequently portrayed as headstrong rebels waging holy war against stodgy and corrupt administrators and broken school systems that have abandoned principles and, indeed, America's students.

In *Freedom Writers*, Hillary Swank buys books and materials that her principal won't purchase and holds life-affirming discussions against the administration's wishes. Michelle Pfeifer dedicates herself to her underprivileged class when the rest of her school has given up on them in the movie *Dangerous Minds*. Even in a film like *The Nutty Professor*, the audience giddily watches Eddie Murphy portray a gentle classroom genius tormented by a college dean so contemptible and vile we feel a sense of glee when a mouse turd drops into his coffee.

And, of course, Robin Williams's classic performance as the iconoclastic teacher John Keating—based loosely on the real-life classroom antics and techniques of Samuel F. Pickering Jr.—motivated and inspired an entire generation of idealistic educators. The movie *Dead Poet's Society* set the bar for teachers who saw staid conformity in their administration's caustic caution.

Unlike Keating, Pickering was neither chased from campus in disgrace nor feted by students standing on their desks as a shocked and grumpy administrator looked on appalled. Pickering left Montgomery Bell Academy in Nashville, Tennessee, on good terms. "Whatever of me is in that character," Pickering told a reporter in 1989, "has got to be small."[1]

An unconventional teacher deciding to leave a school on his own volition doesn't fit the Hollywood narrative of tye-dyed educators struggling against plaid administrators.

In spite of these tropes, an adversarial relationship between teachers and administrators is not given. One of the most attractive aspects of teaching has always been the relative freedom the job allowed, though, and often there is an inherent tension between this freedom and the oversight of an administrator. As state and federal bureaucrats have added mountains of directives, "standards," and benchmarks to the teacher's already overwhelming workload, this tension has increased. But even before the government stepped in, the role of the administrator was always there in a teacher's life.

This relationship is too often overlooked in teacher preparation programs. There are few (if any) courses dedicated to helping teachers coexist with their supervisor. This is a monumental oversight. It is woefully Pollyanna and almost criminally naïve to fail to acknowledge the important place an administrator may occupy relative to a teacher's success or failure. This chapter is about four common types of school administrators and ways to effectively work with them. The hope is to offer practical suggestions so that a teacher can succeed, if necessary, in spite of her boss.

Postman and Weingartner have memorably defined an administrator as "another curious consequence of a bureaucracy which has forgotten its reason for being."[2] I am using the term "administrator" here as a kind of catchall for the myriad roles a supervisor may take in a school setting. Our society is enamored with hierarchies and bureaucracies, so that leadership roles (and to a dangerous sense accountability) are widely dispersed. In this chapter, the term "administrator" may mean a grade-level team leader, a "school" director (elementary, middle, or secondary), or the more traditional school principal.

The four composite administrators, of course, should not be viewed as an all-encompassing description of all types of supervisors, though I believe they will serve as a valuable resource and guide for new teachers. There are administrators who are a combination of several of these categories, and there are also administrators who are in a category all their own—for good or bad.

With that caveat up front, the four types discussed in this chapter are the *Micromanager*, *Captain Hands Off*, the *Super Admin*, and the *God Send*. Each type comes with its own benefits and drawbacks. Most importantly for a new teacher, each type can be worked with and none is a guarantor of success or failure.

The Micromanager

Teachers both good and great are artists. Those who deny this deny the very essence of education, and artists throughout human history have chafed under direction. Charlie Chaplin was only halfway through filming *The Great Dictator* when he began receiving frantic telegrams from United Artists—the American censors were eager to shred his film, England seemed unlikely to even allow it to be screened (desperately hoping to avoid provoking Hitler), and the whole project, including $2,000,000 of Chaplin's own money, seemed doomed to failure. He, however, "was determined to go ahead, for Hitler must be laughed at," he recalled in his autobiography.[3]

Chaplin was so concerned about violence at the film's premiere that he sought help from the Longshoremen's Union for security. But he "was determined to ridicule [the Nazi's] mystic bilge about a pure-blooded race."[4] FDR confidante Harry Hopkins bluntly told Chaplin that the film, though a noble gesture, was destined to lose money. He was wrong, of course, but it is Chaplin the determined, myopic *artist's* steadfast and stubborn refusal to be deterred that is most reminiscent of the character of great educators.

Eleven years before his breakout as space pirate Han Solo, twenty-two-year-old Harrison Ford's one-line performance in 1966's *Dead Heat* got the aspiring actor noticed by a studio executive. In the wrong way, "He called me into his office," Ford recalled in 1984, "and said, 'I want to tell you a story, kid.' Kid, he always called me kid. He was about 15 minutes older than I was . . . He said, 'First time Tony Curtis was ever in a movie . . . he delivered a bag of groceries, a bag of groceries, kid. And you took one look at that guy, and you knew *that* was a movie star.'"[5]

Not one to suffer fools lightly or meekly, Ford shot back, "Well I thought *that* was supposed to be a busboy."[6] An artistic temperament can be difficult and headstrong. It is also this artistic temperament that makes the Micromanager the most difficult supervisor with whom to deal. Under the ever-watchful eye of the micromanaging supervisor, the freedom that is a necessary and inherent part of a teacher's work is severely curtailed. The Micromanager believes that there is one correct way to do everything—and it is always *their* way.

The good news is this is where all that mindless lesson-planning training you have received in your teacher preparation courses will actually come in handy. This kind of administrator, by definition, demands to be included and kept apprised of everything going on within the classroom. It is not uncommon for a Micromanager to ask to see a week's lesson plan and, even more incredibly, she may actually read them.

The Micromanager is a loud proponent of *theory*. These are the folks who read all those education journals written by professors; and these folks take everything they read to heart. Because of their heavy-handed approach to supervision, this becomes an issue for their faculty. One week the administrator reads in a well-respected journal that studies have conclusively shown that children learn better in a cooperative environment, and that the best way to create such an environment is to arrange the desks in a circle. The next morning a memo is awaiting every teacher in the school instructing them to arrange their desks in such a circle.

The faculty, knowing that this is likely a phase, complies while grumbling and rolling their eyes. Three weeks later, this same administrator reads in another journal that the first journal's conclusive findings weren't exactly conclusive after all. It turns out what kids need is a stable structure, and the new study conclusively shows that desks should be arranged in the traditional rows of yesteryear. The next morning, a new memo is awaiting the faculty.

The above example is but one facetious example of what a teacher working with a Micromanager faces. Over time, resentment builds as teachers rightly feel they are not being treated as either adults or professionals. The Micromanager provides an extension of the anger that many teachers feel toward their preparation programs—as both seem to deny the importance of their voices and want them to merely parrot an accepted dogma. Perrone warned, "Turning teachers into technicians, intermediaries for someone else's ideas and curriculum" is poor policy.[7]

Micromanagers view their teachers as technicians designed to carry out their vision, and this negation of the teachers' talents and values can lead to disaster and is certainly not conducive to positive relationships. Professional development under a Micromanager is often particularly galling for teachers. These in-services, which extend the day for already emotionally taxed and exhausted faculty members, are little more than attempts to make the faculty into clones of the administrator. They are not forums for intellectual give and take or even, sadly, true professional growth.

The result is often stunning for a new faculty member, watching in disbelief as veteran teachers congregate as far from the front of the room as possible, and then proceed to pass notes to one another, talk and giggle, doodle, and are exceptionally rude to the guest speaker. The faculty act worse than most of our classrooms ever dreamed of being.

This passive-aggressive revolt comes because the faculty understand what the afternoon session was really about—someone coming in to validate the *theory of the moment* of our fearless (and feckless) leader. The veterans will have none of it; but since required to attend, they sabotage the attempt at further brainwashing by acting childish toward the poor speaker, who leaves wondering just what on earth she did to infuriate the faculty. The quiet rebellion could have been avoided, of course, if only once the administrator asked the faculty what kind of help is needed or what *we* want to learn.

Most teachers would tear down the door of the library to attend any seminar that would make them feel less technologically inadequate. Instead, hours of our lives are wasted listening to vapid consultants "teach" us how to write a meaningful mission statement. It's truly a wonder these consultants aren't torn limb from limb by restless and insulted educators (if only our backs weren't so sore from moving the desks back and forth). The Micromanager is not here to hear.

There is nothing wrong, of course, with accountability to a supervisor. The problem with a micromanaging administrator is the apparent and actual contempt they feel and exhibit the abilities and the ideas of those who work with them. Edicts from "on-high" will not provide a teacher with the needed inspiration to succeed. Rather, it contributes to the burnout of the creative and imaginative teachers we are losing each year as the teacher shortage crisis deepens and spreads across the land. There are some survival strategies for working with a Micromanager that can help you survive and thrive, though, even as he looks over your shoulder.

First, under no circumstances try to out-theorize these folks. In North Carolina we call this "hollerin' down a rain barrel." That means it is a useless exercise. The Micromanager's theoretical foundation is typically transitory anyway, so even a successful attempt recruiting them to your way of thinking wouldn't last. More important is the fact that they believe they know more than their faculty, so discourse is unlikely. Second, learn well the art of subterfuge. That is to say the teacher must understand the need to exist on two levels simultaneously—the administrator's and his own.

Although an educator's freedoms are greatly curtailed in our current climate, it remains true that when the door closes it is still the teacher's room. Smile at the directives and the incessant memos and then, as much as possible, do your own thing to the absolute best of your ability. Moving the desks is a pain, but it is unlikely to alter your ability to reach and teach a child.

Since the Micromanager is focused on minutia most of the time, provide superficial acquiescence. Finally, and perhaps most importantly, build and cultivate relationships with your students' parents and guardians. Developing a (deserved) reputation among parents as a good teacher who cares about and works tirelessly for and with students provides a teacher freedom from the whims of an administrator that is far more valuable than tenure ever could be.

There is a slight silver lining to working with the Micromanager. Like the proverbial broken clock that is correct twice a day, there is a positive lesson that can be drawn from the Micromanager. While it can be grating, the level of involvement they demand and the level of communication they ask for is never, ever a bad idea, no matter what sort of supervisor you encounter. Ensuring that your administrator is "in the loop" and aware of what's going on within your classroom is always the right move, because all administrators despise surprises.

Communication is the heart of all relationships, professional and personal, and maintaining open lines to the office and the administration is, cynically, a way to keep your behind covered and, idealistically, a way to showcase your classroom and your students. In either interpretation or a healthy mixture of the two, communication is paramount.

Captain Hands Off

The advisor was flustered and frustrated. It was embarrassingly, painfully obvious that the briefing book had not been cracked open the night before. The president was woefully unprepared as he headed to that afternoon's summit—a gathering of global leaders dedicated to plotting out the future of the world's economy. No big deal. Seeing the disappointment on his aide's face, President Ronald Reagan sheepishly admitted, "Well, Jim . . . *The Sound of Music* was on last night."[8] Later, Reagan quipped that his seat in the cabinet room would be memorialized with a plaque reading, "Reagan Slept Here."[9]

This charming hands-off attitude brought the nation the Iran-Contra scandal and a wildly corrupt presidential administration. Ronald Reagan is a perfect mascot for our next type of administrator, Captain Hands Off. The polar opposite of the Micromanager, her mantra is, "I trust my faculty." While this sounds wonderful in theory, in practice it too often simply translates as *you* do all the work. This supervisor is the absolute master of delegation. The answer to nearly every issue is to develop a committee to "look into it."

Two teachers approach the principal with their concern that some of the high-school students are vaping in the school restroom. Rather than deal with the issue at hand, this administrator names the two teachers as cochairs of the new Faculty Committee on Rest Room Vaping. Six years and thousands of donuts later, students are still vaping away. The Committee on Committees is, after all, a real thing.

The central operating factor for Captain Hands Off is putting enough distance between himself and all sides of all angles of all issues in order to have what the US government calls "plausible deniability." Unlike the Micromanager, this administrator is far more comfortable *not* knowing what goes on in your classroom. The greatest frustration for teachers working with Captain Hands Off is with their definition of success and failure, and the sharing of responsibility.

To the great frustration and consternation of teachers, Captain Hands Off defines success in terms that are purely transactional. A new teacher begins an afterschool drama club. This club works and struggles and commits and eventually produces a spring production of *Oklahoma!* On Opening Night, Captain Hands Off has one of two reactions: If the auditorium is packed to the rafters and the production is a success, he will gladly tell anyone who will listen how he knew this was a great idea and that he knew all along that it was going to be a great, tremendous, stupendous success. He will even imply that he had hung around the school during all those late nights and helped out in some way.

The teacher listens to all this while gnawing a whole in her tongue, because she knows she hasn't seen or heard from Captain Hands Off since the day she approached him for permission to attempt the play. If only a few stragglers come to the show, kids forget lines and sets nearly decapitate the trombone player, then he will whisper to other faculty and parents that he had not really supported the idea all along and felt the teacher was being too ambitious in her goal of bringing a Broadway musical to Smalltown, USA.

As with the Micromanager, there are survival strategies for a new teacher to use to succeed when working with Captain Hands Off. The first is to know your boundaries well. When working with Captain Hands Off, you will have fewer resources and less support than many other teachers. That can't be a surprise to you. Don't feign surprise when she does not come to rehearsals for the play. This is something that you should have been aware of before the first song was played on the school's out-of-key piano.

When working with this type of administrator, the best thing for a teacher to do is to make the most of the freedom afforded. These administrators are duly famous for sequestering themselves in their offices and venturing out into classrooms and the hallways as frequently as Punxsutawney Phil. For the new teacher this means that, unlike working with the Micromanager, you are not being kept on a short leash. Let loose that torrent of idealism and creativity you have had stored away during all those years of formal schooling.

A second strategy for succeeding with a Captain Hands Off is to provide food at any function where you truly need or want their attendance (this also works with raccoons). A bag of chips, some soda, and a case of Dixie cups never fail to get these folks out of their undisclosed location. If you are meeting with a group of parents or students and want to make sure that your supervisor is aware of the hours and the sweat that you are pouring into a project (whether curricular or extra), make sure your note to her mentions food.

Finally, whether a new or a veteran teacher, you should feel *positively no guilt* if your work makes Captain Hands Off work hard(er). If he has to come unlock the school on a Saturday morning for you and your students, so be it. If he is needed as a chaperone for a field trip or a dance, again, so be it. It is not your problem if your work is making this individual step up and do his job.

Super Administrator

The Apostle Paul was full of blunt candor when he described the lengths to which he would go to win souls for Christ in his letter to the church at Corinth. "To the Jews," he unashamedly admitted,

> I became as a Jew, in order to win Jews. To those under the law I became as one under the law . . . so that I might win those under the law. . . . To the weak, I became weak, so that I might win the weak. I have become all things to all people.

There is no better description of our next type of supervisor, the Super Administrator, than Paul's *all things to all people.*

This sounds like the kind of supervisor we would all want to have, right? Hardly, the Super Administrator has great intentions, but the results are often chaos, resentment, and confusion. These poor souls desperately *want* to be all things to all people. They are more interested in being liked than in being respected, and that makes them weak leaders. They are poor decision-makers, and often stretched too thin in their work and their commitments. These are the administrators who leave the school every evening around nine o'clock and are always back the next morning at six. The reason for this is, of course, that they cannot say the word "no" to anyone.

The result of this neediness is that you can never depend on them. I once had a Super Administrator, three fellow teachers, and a great row over $87 that was somehow unclaimed in the budget. I went to Super Administrator first and asked for the money to be used for a drama production. No problem, he said. I mistakenly told another teacher about this windfall, and she marched to his office demanding the money for the foreign language club. No problem, he said. A third teacher got into the act over a new dry-erase board. Again, no problem.

In the end, I have no idea who received the money (it wasn't me), but I am sure that it came down not to the validity of the claim, but on who got to Super Administrator last. This is no way to run a school, or anything else for that matter, and the lack of firm decisions always erodes the faculty's confidence in the administrator and often in themselves.

To survive and thrive when working with a Super Administrator, a teacher must do several things. First, always understand that these people are fragile. Yes, some Super Administrators are dishonest people, but overwhelmingly (I believe) they are well-intentioned folks who simply have a preternatural need to be liked by all. It is also important to understand that this need will likely lead the Super Administrator to tell you whatever it is she thinks you want to hear, so take it with a HUGE grain of salt. When she tells you that you are the best sixth-grade teacher she has ever seen, don't be surprised to learn she said the same thing about the previous two sixth-grade teachers.

You may be a phenomenal educator, but don't believe it based solely on her words. A new teacher working with a Super Administrator also needs to utilize other faculty members whenever possible if she wants to grow and develop in her work. An observation by Super Administrator is going to end up telling you how great you are; such pithy reports won't help you grow. Therefore, ask a veteran teacher whom you respect to come in occasionally and observe your teaching so that you might get some constructive and useful feedback.

Finally, do not depend on Super Administrator no matter how enthusiastic he may seem about your work. Always know that you are being told what he assumes you want to hear, therefore don't be shocked if the support is not there when the time comes. Although my experience has been that Super Administrators mean well, the outcomes are not productive or conducive to education.

The God Send

Exhausted and humiliated, John F. Kennedy, in office only three months, stared out, hollow-eyed, at the gathered reporters. Glumly, he shouldered the blame—all of it—for the Bay of Pigs debacle. There was no equivocation or deflection. Months later, the chastened president met privately with the journalist Hugh Sidey and urged him to write a book on the disaster. "I want to know how all this could have happened," Kennedy said.[10] "There were 50 or so of us, presumably the most experienced and smartest people we could get, to plan such an operation. Most of us thought it would work."[11]

It was the groupthink, and how as a leader he could have gotten sucked into it, that haunted Kennedy. He continued,

> five minutes after it began to fall in, we all looked at each other and asked, 'How could we have been so stupid?' When we saw the wide range of the failures we asked ourselves why it had not been apparent to somebody from the start. I guess you get walled off from reality when you want something to succeed too much. Remember, Sidey, write that book and explain it to all of us.[12]

In many ways, President John Kennedy's performance was exemplary of the last type of administrator, the God Send. Responsibility, accountability, a desire and willingness to understand what went wrong, and measures to improve, all are characteristics of strong leaders. Obviously, his performance was far from perfect—the entire operation ended in bloody disaster.

However, the God Send administrator is not perfect; no one is. Searching for perfection is useless and dreadfully unfair to our supervisor. Mistakes will be made, there will be disagreements—some vehement—regarding policy and other matters. Miscommunication can and will happen. Differences of opinion will occur and decisions—tough ones—will be made.

With the God Send faculty may not always get their way, but they will always know they have been *heard*. The God Send's characteristics read in many ways like clichés of leadership. They are tough, dependable, respected, fair, and supportive. They are open to the ideas of others, although that does not mean they will always accept your ideas. This type of administrator does her work exceedingly well. If she has a drawback, it is that she is utterly intolerant of laziness or pettiness (and that hardly seems like a drawback).

They are impatient with fools. They expect the same level of commitment from their faculty that they themselves bring to the table. They exhibit an active respect for their faculty—more than mere lip service or smokescreens. Active respect is challenging and not passive, allowing and requiring teachers to be responsible and professional practitioners and not puppets of pet theories.

The God Send understands the twin existence of every great teacher as scholar and practitioner, and respects and cultivates individual experience and talent among her faculty rather than seeking replication of some preordained notion of what a teacher must be. It is honesty and respect, not perfection, that characterize the God Send administrator the most.

One of the ugliest and most unfortunate legacies of the high-stakes era of education is the stoking of the tension between administrators and teachers. In this era, it seems the relationship is characterized more by the need of supervisors to impose accountability than to assist teachers in growing and developing in the profession. Punishment, not cooperation, is the sad new paradigm. Efforts to divide and conquer have been all too successful. Teachers and administrators are not destined for conflict, however.

There are terrific educational leaders among us and all around us, and equally important for a new teacher, you can truly be successful with every single type of administrator with whom you may work. All relationships come with challenges, ebbs and flows. Whoever our supervisor is, in the final analysis we will determine our own legacy.

Notes

1. *Times Daily*, Associated Press. "Real-life Professor Inspires 'Dead Poets' Character." July 10, 1989, 4B.

2. Neil Postman and Charles Weingartner, *Teaching as a Subversive Activity: A No-holds-barred Assault on Outdated Teaching Methods—with Dramatic and Practical Proposals on How Education can be Made Relevant to Today's World* (New York: Delacorte Press, 1969), p. 153.

3. Charles Chaplin, *My Autobiography* (New York: Simon and Schuster, 1964), p. 392.

4. Chaplin, *My Autobiography*, pp. 392–393.

5. Ryan Parker, "Harrison Ford Once Joked the Studio Executive Who Disliked His First Film Became His Butler." *The Hollywood Reporter*, July 13, 2016. Retrieved from https://www.hollywoodreporter.com/heat-vision/harrison-ford-birthday-star-joked-910573, February 11, 2020.

6. Parker, "Harrison Ford Once Joked."

7. Vito Perrone, *A Letter to Teachers: Reflections on Schooling and the Art of Teaching* (San Francisco, CA: Jossey Bass, 1991), p. 80.

8. William Leuchtenburg, "Behind the Ronald Reagan Myth: 'No one had ever entered the White House so grossly ill informed'." *Salon*, December 28, 2015. Retrieved from https://www.salon.com/2015/12/27/behind_the_ronald_reagan_myth_no_one_had_ever_entered_the_white_house_so_grossly_ill_informed_2/, February 11, 2020.

9. Leuchtenburg, "Behind the Ronald Reagan Myth."

10. Hugh Sidey, "The Lesson John Kennedy Learned from the Bay of Pigs." *Time*, April 16, 2001. Retrieved from http://content.time.com/time/nation/article/0,8599,106537,00.html, February 11, 2020.

11. Sidey, "The Lesson John Kennedy Learned."

12. Sidey, "The Lesson John Kennedy Learned."

CHAPTER 5

~

The Same River Twice

This chapter is not about educational theory; it is about educational philosophy. To borrow from Mark Twain, the difference is like that between the lightening and the lightening bug. An educational philosophy must encompass the teacher's "views about reality, knowledge, and values, together with a perspective on the nature of humankind and its society."[1] It is how we view life, our role in the world, our hopes, dreams, and even fears for the future. Our educational philosophy frames how we view our students and the community in which we work, as well as how we define ourselves as teacher, leader, and citizen.

Our educational theory, which we shall examine in the next chapter, is our philosophy in action, our *praxis*. This philosophy is not static and will adapt and change throughout a teacher's career. It is not one of those mission statement exercises to be done and placed on a shelf, but should be the beating heart of our daily decisions and practice. Evans writes, "A philosophy of education is only useful to educators if it enlarges our understanding of learning, shows relationships of persons, ideas, and things, and is based on concrete appreciation of whatever is being considered."[2]

Our educational philosophy holds our best and most cherished ideals and ideas, and Mesle reminds us that "ideas shape actions, so it matters how we think about reality, the world, and ourselves."[3] For too many pre-service teachers, once the dreaded word "theory" is seen there is a reflexive desire to move on. Many have been bombarded with difficult-to-pronounce names and strange theories that never seem to connect with the practice you envision for your classroom.

That is a major problem, because philosophy and theory have their place and importance. When they appear divorced from practice and practicality, however, these crucial ideals lose their meaning. Thus, many pre-service teachers leave their training programs resentful of and antagonistic toward the very idea of educational philosophy.

Our philosophy is based on the metaphysics of Alfred North Whitehead, the ideals of John Dewey, and the cosmology of Hazrat Inayat Khan. In such that labels are useful, our philosophy is one of construction and one of process. How to best describe the philosophy? Marie Shear famously quipped that feminism is the radical notion that women are people and, for our purposes, this philosophy revolves around the equally radical notion that *children* are people. Whitehead once emphatically told his gathered students, "Educate yourselves. No one else can do it for you. You are not pieces of clay which clever teachers are molding" into their proper shape.[4]

John Dewey wrote that "the aim of education is to enable individuals to continue their education—or . . . [for] continued capacity for growth."[5] Perrone has written that "engaging the students means taking them seriously, acknowledging that they are trying to understand the world in which they live and that what is studied in school must make connections to that underlying intention."[6] This respect for the agency of children and young people as well as their natural curiosity and imagination are the cornerstone of this philosophy—our insistent view that children are, indeed, people. Our construction/process philosophy has three parts: a disposition of *humility*, a requirement of *interest*, and an outcome of *wisdom*.

Disposition: Humility

Alfred North Whitehead was a British mathematician and a philosopher who became deeply intrigued by the way we learn. This fascination was natural and familial. Born in 1861 in East Kent near the Channel, the frail Whitehead—youngest of Alfred and Sarah Whitehead's four children—was born into a family of educators and clergy. His father was an Anglican priest who homeschooled young Alfred and brought him along during his frequent visits to his rural parish's three parochial schools.[7]

His own classroom career began when he was named as a teaching fellow at Cambridge University in 1884, and his observations of and views on teaching and learning were published as *The Aims of Education and Other Essays* in 1929. Whitehead's notions of education focus more on who the student is than on what the teacher should do, and are part of his larger philosophy, which Whitehead termed as "process philosophy." It is in this philosophy of process that we are provided the necessary humility for our own educational philosophy to work.

At the heart of process theory is the idea that the essence of reality, the only constant, is a change. Many process philosophers trace their thought back to Heraclitus and his famous aphorism that you cannot step into the same river twice. When we speak of process in this sense, we "are not considering procedures, but something that is connected with the idea of becoming."[8] Whitehead wrote, "Advance or Decadence are the only choices offered to mankind. The pure conservative is fighting against the essence of the universe."[9]

This denial of a static reality holds the promise of keeping educators humble because it is a reminder that, as Dylan told us, those not busy being born are busy dying. Mesle notes what he calls Whitehead's "bold humility," his insistence on always questioning and progressing in our thoughts and practice. Whitehead left no doubt as to his feelings about those who claimed philosophic certainty: "In philosophical discussion," he wrote, "the merest hint of dogmatic certainty . . . is an exhibition of folly."[10]

Teachers know both intuitively and experientially that the lesson plan that works to perfection in first period might fall flat in fourth period. In process theory, the primacy of change keeps us from turning our classroom theories and practices into "dogmatic certainty." In his lecture entitled "The Rhythmic Claims of Freedom and Discipline," Whitehead warned, "Education is a difficult problem, to be solved by no one simple formula."[11] We are humble before the diversity and uniqueness of our students, knowing that our goal is not ideological or philosophical purity but *their* best learning environment.

Dewey scolds, "It is not enough that certain materials and methods have proved effective with other individuals at other times. There must be a reason for thinking that they will function in generating an experience that has educative quality" in the present for our current students.[12] Process theory offers neither the illusion of finality nor the comfort of certainty. We are on a journey as teachers, and the myth of the one-size-fits-all theory of education must be abandoned. In process philosophy, Whitehead reminds us all that, "Life in the real world, the concrete experience of human beings, denies acceptance of absolutes."[13]

Whitehead's process philosophy also demands humility because it does no less than require teachers raised and practicing in our Western, materialist model of schooling to radically reimagine schools and, indeed, the world. Process theory views our society and our existence as "a web of interrelated processes of which we are integral parts, so that all of our choices and actions have consequences for the world around us."[14] This worldview sees connectedness and relationships as integral to understanding society. Whitehead believed "that everything in this world is in some way connected with every other thing in this world" according to process philosopher Malcolm D. Evans.[15]

The importance for teachers is the much-needed replacement of our current model of competition and rabid individualism with "a construct of *individual in community*," Evans continues.[16] Dewey also noted that relationships and community are vital in the school system of a democracy, writing, "a community or social group sustains itself through continuous self-renewal" accomplished through education.[17] He was deeply frustrated that his writings had been misinterpreted and twisted to fit America's fetishizing of the individual: "Why do writers and teachers insist on saddling me with the 'child-centered' school?" he wearily asked. "Anyone who has read me knows that it is the socially centered school that I have sought."[18]

Helping our students realize how their actions and decisions impact those around them—the symbiotic nature of living in a republic—teaches them individual *and* communal responsibility. Perrone writes:

> Education at its best is always about democracy. That belief dominated Dewey's thought. After all, school was about living in the world, learning to be in a position to remake the society. What good is an education if it doesn't contribute to making one's community a better place to live, if it doesn't enhance the potential for productive relationships, if it doesn't cause us to understand others more constructively, or if it doesn't produce greater integrity? As Elie Weisel points out often, the Nazi SS were graduates of Germany's best universities. What was the quality of their moral education? According to Dewey, education was most productive when its starting point was the needs that existed in the local community—when it was about transformation and improvement of the society.[19]

Paulo Freire has written, "Education, as a specifically human experience, is a form of intervention in the world."[20] For the teacher, process philosophy is democratic education. We are an interdependent planet now more than ever, and our educational philosophy should reflect this truth or we risk becoming twenty-first-century Luddites.

"Mankind is interdependent," Khan wrote, "and the happiness of each depends upon the happiness of all, and it is this lesson that humanity has to learn today as the first and the last lesson."[21] Education that reflects our relationships and draws connections to the world is also a relevant education. We have too many sacred cows in the teaching profession. We teach too many topics because they have always been taught, without thinking about whether or not these topics are truly relevant in the students' lives.

But common sense instructs us that material which is not seen as useful by a student will not be learned. A student has no business accepting that material is crucial to their world and their future because we say so—they are not robots, after all. We must prove a topic's usefulness, and this is best accomplished by teaching a relevant curriculum that is connected to and deepened by the world of our students—local and global.

Whitehead's process theory necessitates humility for teachers, finally, in its demand that education strike a balance between freedom and discipline, and the role this requires of teachers. "Freedom and discipline," Whitehead wrote, "are the two essentials of education."[22] In a similar vein, Khan wrote, "What a youth needs most is not encouragement; what he needs most is balance."[23] The teacher in our philosophy has a crucial role to play in the education of students, but must remain mindful that she is only one aspect of a child's education.

An essential characteristic of a teacher's role in process theory is acknowledging, honoring, and employing the natural curiosity of youth and children by providing the necessary freedom for wonder to explore and expand. Think here of the old saying, "You can lead a horse to water, but you cannot make the horse drink." A teacher's job is to remind his students that they are, indeed, thirsty. A teacher need not instill curiosity or inquisitiveness into our pupils. Anyone who has spent even a nanosecond with a child knows full well that children are naturally curious beings—far more so than adults, sadly.

Proof of this can be found in the fact that there is an industry devoted to manufacturing covers for electrical outlets in homes. Too many children have wondered, "What happens when I stick my finger in the wall?" Too often education destroys or binds this sense of wonder, and in Whitehead's inimitable phrase, "Cursed be the dullard who destroys wonder."[24] The trouble is that education is not set up in this nation in a way that takes full advantage of the curiosity of children and young people. In fact, the polar opposite is the case. Our system sets up roadblocks to the imagination and inquisitiveness of a child.

"We deprive the children of their freedom," Inayat Khans despairs,

> Of the time which they ought to have at home to play and to think little and enjoy life more, and to keep away from worries and anxieties. We take away that best time in life of a child by sending it to school.[25]

This duality—school or freedom—is, however, a false choice. It will often be the job of the teacher to guide and encourage this curiosity, but she must not kill the initiative of the student by exerting too much control. Dewey says,

To talk about an educational aim when approximately each act of a pupil is dictated by the teacher, when the only order in the sequence of his acts is that which comes from the assignment of lessons and the giving of directions by another, is to talk nonsense.[26]

We must be humble enough to remember that we are but one piece of the puzzle. Inayat Khan provides a note of humility for educators when he reminds us, "As the Brahmin says, the first Guru is the mother, the second Guru is the father, and the third Guru is the teacher."[27] Dewey wrote, "What conscious, deliberate teaching can do is at most to free the capacities" our students bring with them from their environments outside our classroom and control.[28] To free the capacities of our students means to free them to the limitless horizon of their own curiosity.

Still, the teacher matters. Process theory does not reduce the teacher to a glorified babysitter. Our job is still vital to the process. A teacher's role is not that of a dictator but rather that of a fellow traveler engaged with her students in the search for meaning. Discipline during this search is crucial, because as Khan reminds us, "If the spirit of freedom becomes destructive it loses the essence of democracy."[29]

A teacher sets up the lesson by introducing the topic at hand, but then works with her students in a process that seeks to make that topic meaningful. Whitehead writes, "The dominant note of education at its beginning and at its end is freedom, but . . . there is an intermediate stage of discipline with freedom in subordination."[30]

Students need discipline to channel their wonder; students need discipline to weigh competing evidence; students need discipline because of "the inescapable fact that there are right ways and wrong ways, and definite truths to be known" according to Whitehead.[31] A thoughtful, skillful educator is especially necessary as students integrate new information and synthesize experience with thought. John Dewey's description of the teacher's role is in agreement with process philosophy's: "The alternative to furnishing ready-made subject matter and listening to the accuracy with which it is reproduced is not quiescence, but participation, sharing, in an activity."[32]

Whitehead's description of how a university professor should present himself applies equally to a K-12 educator: "as an ignorant man thinking, actively utilizing his small share of knowledge."[33] We model freedom by remaining curious; we model discipline by maintaining intellectual honesty. The disposition required to know when each is required and in what measure is humility, the very-high-standard process theory sets for us all.

Whitehead's focus on the necessary balance between freedom for the students' curious natures and the discipline required to transform wonder into knowledge, as well as his insistence on the connectedness of all our efforts and existence, calls for humble educators journeying with their students to unknown and unknowable destinations.

Requirement: Interest

It is no surprise that John Dewey's view of education revolved around social responsibilities and our relationships and responsibilities to one another. Dewey spent much of his life living for others, progressing, as his biographer notes, from "living for his parents first and for others later, until eventually he committed himself to representing the needs of the American people."[34] Born two years before Whitehead, October 20, 1859, John Dewey was a replacement child. Ten months before John's birth, his parents lost their youngest child, also named John, in a horrific accident. Dewey grew up aware of the loss as well as his role in his parents' new world.

His biographer writes,

> Most of us live and act for others as well as ourselves. But replacement children inherit a duty to live not just for themselves and their parents but for the lost child as well. They have to bear anxieties in their parents that for a long time they cannot understand and perhaps never will understand.[35]

It is an extraordinary burden to feel your life is not your own, that your life is another's legacy, and to have the shadow of tragedy looming like bad weather over every accomplishment. For Dewey, it meant grounding both his life and his philosophy into one of the service and connection, and for educators it means viewing education as preparation for and practice of an active, participatory democratic society.

Dewey certainly would have agreed with Khan, who wrote, "On the education of children depends the future of nations."[36] In practice, in our classrooms mean respecting students and treating them like sentient, thoughtful, and capable beings. No more *tabula rasa*. Our students' interests, backgrounds, aspirations, and needs will be taken into account in everything we do. Dewey wrote,

> There is no such thing as educational value in the abstract. The notion that some subjects and methods and that acquaintance with certain facts and truths possess educational value in and of themselves is the reason why traditional

education reduced the material of education so largely to a diet of predigested materials.[37]

Handing down education like a family heirloom will not work; Dewey demands we provide a useful, relevant curriculum to our young ones. And he denies that we may require their attention or take their time on the thin gruel of tradition or "because I said so." In this he was in agreement with Whitehead. One of Whitehead's most famous sayings is "the students are alive," and process theory demands students be viewed as Dewey would have wanted us to see them, as individual children with agency and experience.[38] For Whitehead, this meant extending respect to our students by not taking their interest for granted, and, as he insisted, "Interest is the *sine qua non* for attention and apprehension."[39]

Process theory holds as a fundamental ideal that you cannot teach a child without first getting that child interested in the material you are presenting. "There can be no mental development without interest," Whitehead emphatically states.[40] In case there were any doubt, he repeated within the same paragraph, "Without interest there will be no progress."[41] Mesle writes that this foundational principle "demands that we take seriously the embodiment of children."[42]

In process philosophy, a teacher's role is not to transmit knowledge but to awaken a desire, to stimulate a disposition, toward learning. "The most important attitude," education can cultivate, according to Dewey, "is that of desire to go on learning."[43] To ignore the role of interest is to inculcate an attitude of passivity and submission in our students. "We cannot educate for democracy and fascism simultaneously," Evans warns darkly.[44]

A teacher cannot arouse the interest of her students, however, if she does not know her students. To know what is likely to ignite a spark within our students requires a kind of knowing that is too often ignored in teacher preparation programs. This is a knowing beyond last year's test scores or the reading level group of our students. This is about knowing our students as living beings. Perrone writes that teaching "is about *knowing* children well."[45] Keeping foremost in our thoughts the understanding that our children are far more than clay to be manipulated or replaceable cogs in a machine, a student "viewed from a process perspective is a student viewed holistically.

Teachers do not confront a mind, or a body, or cognition, or affect, but, a totality; learners bring their whole being to the situation" of learning.[46] Khan argued that the education of children should include five "points of view: physical, mental, moral, social, and spiritual."[47] Whitehead was clear in his respect for the vital importance of experience and all that the learner brings with himself into the classroom. He wrote, "The ancient doctrine that 'no one crosses the same river twice' is extended. No thinker thinks twice; and, to put the matter more generally, no subject experiences twice."[48]

In *Experience and Education*, Dewey wrote,

> It is a cardinal precept of the newer school of education that the beginning of instruction shall be made with the experience learners already have; that this experience and the capacities that have been developed during its course provide the starting point for all further learning.[49]

We cannot possibly make the experiences of our students the starting point of our pedagogy, however, if we have not invested the time and effort to know what these experiences are.

We must lose forever the absurd attitude that students walk into our classrooms as blank slates upon which we will write certain information or beliefs. The idea that a student leaves behind all they have experienced once the door to the classroom closes is utter foolishness. A student comes into our classroom with worries and troubles and hopes just the same as an adult would. Perhaps, they fear a terrorist attack. Maybe they are concerned because Mom or Dad has lost his or her job. A student might be worried about a neighbor who is trying to sell him drugs. Such experience is a part of the intellectual and emotional fabric of a student, and we ignore them at our peril.

In process theory, an educator does not ignore or deny a student's world and experience, we use them to further the aims of education. Perrone writes,

> When teachers know their students well—their interests, learning patterns, general stance, the meaning of their gestures, their ways of approaching new materials and fresh ideas, and their outlook on the world—they can more productively engage them on a personal basis, ensuring a deeper entry into learning.[50]

In other words, as process theory demands, we can pique the students' interest.

A student's worldview will be the foundation upon which they will construct their future opinions and knowledge. In process theory, a teacher will strive to provide a classroom environment that values the experiences of students, as well as provides *new* experiences for students to rethink and question their attitudes and values. Our job is not to provide experiences that will change a student's value system. That is not education—it is indoctrination. Process theory provides students the freedom to question their (and our) presumptions and assumptions.

Through the questioning, a student discards false information or beliefs held without adequate information and questioning, or becomes better able to defend their values and beliefs because, having questioned them, they are now stronger. Valuing the experiences of our students does not mean that we do not challenge them. Experience is the foundation upon which our students stand, but it is also a filter through which all material must and does pass.

Once again, the better we know our students, the better we are able to see how experience can translate into biases and shallow beliefs. But we do not deny or belittle the experience. Rather, we provide students with new and challenging experiences that, we hope, can open up their worldview.

Dewey writes, "The only freedom that is of enduring importance is freedom of intelligence, that is to say, freedom of observation and of judgment exercised in behalf of purposes that are intrinsically worthwhile."[51] Process theory places great emphasis on the lived experience of students but does not allow these experiences to be accepted *prima facie* and without intellectually rigorous questioning and examination. Instead, it uses lived experience and then demands its examination so that students may answer the age-old question: *How do you know what you know?*

It is the ability to answer this question, that is, after all, the very essence of intellectual activity and education. According to Whitehead, ignoring the uniqueness of each and every student in favor of a curriculum handed down from the county or state has a sad and predictable outcome: "The production of a plentiful array of dunces."[52] In place of producing dunces, process theory produces individuals comfortable with intellectual discomfort. Khan calls this, simply, as wisdom. "The more wise one becomes," Khan wrote, "the more one is able to contradict one's own ideas."[53]

Outcome: Wisdom

The authorities were deeply skeptical of the Indian man trying to enter the country. He had arrived aboard the Pittsburgh after a tumultuous journey across the Atlantic ("Winds, Waves and Steerage Passengers Who Want to Fight Keep Captain Busy," *The New York Times* blared), and he assured the nervous immigration officials he "had no connection with the ideas of Ghandi."[54] It was February 1923, and although Inayat Khan also assured the media that "he was not interested in politics, [and] therefore he did not care to comment on the status of the Ghandi movement in India," immigration inspectors coldly informed him that the Hindu quota for the month had already been met, and he was unceremoniously deposited at Ellis Island to wait.[55]

The humiliation could not have surprised him, though. His gospel of one world religion with all of humanity in harmony made many Americans nervous, including those in power. He was but one of the Hindu "swamis" called out in a hysterical screed that ran in the *Idaho Statesman* in 1912. The paper's headline declared, "American Women Victims of Hindu Mysticism."[56]

Inayat Khan was described as "a clever exponent of Eastern vocal music" in a movement of "Unprecedented Activity in Proselytizing by Swamis Across the United States [that] Has Caused This Government to Investigate Migration of Converts to India—Women Are Forsaking Fortunes, Homes, Husbands and Children" due to the dangerous teachings being espoused.[57] Though Inayat Khan marveled at the depth of racial animus in America, he never wavered in his belief that humankind could be brought into harmony.

Inayat Khan wrote, "There are two aspects of intelligence: intellect, and wisdom."[58] The Sufi philosopher viewed intellect as being defined by knowledge, but wisdom as the utilization *of* knowledge, so that we may see and understand relationships. For Khan, wisdom is an illuminated knowledge, and it "opens up the sight to the similarity of all things and beings, as well as the unity in names and forms."[59] Whitehead throws both shade and shame when he writes, "In the schools of antiquity philosophers aspired to impart wisdom, in modern colleges our humbler aim is to teach subjects."[60]

Whitehead continues with a true sense of urgency:

> But when ideals have sunk to the level of practice, the result is stagnation. In particular, so long as we conceive intellectual education as merely consisting in the acquirement of mechanical mental aptitudes, and of formulated statements of useful truths, there can be no progress; though there will be much activity.[61]

Like Khan, he believed education's "whole aim is the production of active wisdom," and not the memorization of a litany of disconnected facts.[62] Like Inayat Khan, Whitehead saw wisdom as the utilization of what we know. "The importance of knowledge," he wrote, "lies in its use, in our active mastery of it—that is to say, it lies in wisdom."[63]

In *Adventures of Ideas*, Whitehead memorably defines wisdom as "persistent pursuit of the deeper understanding."[64] For process theory, then, the outcome of a true education will not be knowledge, but wisdom. "A merely well-informed man," Whitehead wrote, "is the most useless bore on God's earth."[65] Process theory insists on the use, the relevance, and the application of knowledge; it is a rejection of what Whitehead called inert ideas "knowledge without use." Speaking of ideas and concepts that we may teach, he said, "The child should make them his own, and should understand their application here and now in the circumstances of his actual life."[66]

Malena Ernman was sure she was losing her daughter, recalling the terror of watching her child "slowly disappearing into some kind of darkness."[67] Greta Thunberg was eleven years old in the fall of 2014, had just begun fifth grade, and appeared to be coming apart at the seams. "She stopped playing the piano," Ernman wrote. "She stopped laughing. She stopped talking. And she stopped eating." Greta cried herself to sleep at night, cried in the morning, cried going to school, and while at school—occasionally becoming so distraught that her father, Svante, was forced to pick her up early and bring her home, where she silently clung to the family pet as the gloom descended, spread, and clung to the child like kudzu.

Malena remembered the nadir, an "evening in the autumn of 2014," when she and Svante "sat slumped on our bathroom floor in Stockholm" exhausted and very nearly devoid of hope or ideas.[68] Shortly after, Greta experienced her first panic attack, a devastating event Malena recalled: "She makes a sound we've never heard before, ever. She lets out an abysmal howl that lasts for over 40 minutes . . . Greta ask[ed], 'Am I going to get well again?'"[69]

At school, Greta's class was shown a film about the amount of trash dumped into the world's oceans. The film depicted "an island of plastic, larger than Mexico" that existed in the South Pacific. She cried again, throughout the movie, but this time it was different. These were tears of fire. When the movie was over the teacher and the class moved on, but Greta did not. The story of the island of garbage had sparked something in her and lit a fire that would, without hyperbole, enlighten the world.

On August 20, 2018, Greta Thunberg, armed with an extra sweater, a cushion, a lunchbox, and hundred flyers she had designed and printed out herself went to the Swedish parliament building and held her first climate strike.[70] "Time is much shorter than we think," she warned. "Failure means disaster."[71] In the time since that first lonely strike Greta has become a symbol of hope and determination for millions across the globe. This heroic child is a powerful example of process theory. The requirement of interest was met through the film—even if accidentally.

That is no surprise—the manufacturing of interest and inspiration will surely be a hit-or-miss prospect. If there were a formula, no lesson would ever fail. Still, in the story of the terrible abuse of the planet, Greta found a cause. We see the disposition of humility in Greta's awe-inspiring parents, who refused to give up on their daughter or to ever sell her short. How many parents would have responded with cold condescension and insouciance when

Greta announced that she wanted to skip school to sit outside of parliament protesting climate change?

How many parents would have counseled their teenage daughter to aim lower, to be more realistic? Too many, to be sure. Greta's parents, however, encouraged and supported her, seeing the new-found purpose in their daughter and what it meant to her. The outcome process theory hopes for—wisdom—is exhibited in Greta's beautiful crusade, in her daily application of the materials she has consumed since that first inspiration during the classroom movie.

She has come to embody wisdom as she travels the globe tirelessly advocating for action to address and confront climate change. Greta has withstood mockery, harassment, and bullying from "adults" who should know better. In the face of such ignorance, Greta has pushed ahead, John the Baptist announcing a new world order to a stubborn world.

Inayat Khan wrote, "There are many illnesses, but hopelessness is the worst illness."[72] We recall Jane Addams's haunting description of the young people she witnessed around her, whose "uselessness hangs about them heavily."[73] There is no uselessness about Greta, only purpose and passion. She is using what she has learned and she is applying the information she has gathered in school and on her own to affect change in her world. And a child shall lead them indeed. As interest, humility, and wisdom intersect in the story of Greta, we see process theory in action.

Those in Greta's life who have supported this growth and change may not consider themselves process philosophers or practitioners, but they allowed the natural cycle of learning to happen. They honored Greta's natural rhythm of learning. Now we will return to Whitehead to develop a theory of education that also asks us to tap into these same cycles.

Notes

1. Malcolm D. Evans, *Whitehead and Philosophy of Education: The Seamless Coat of Learning* (Amsterdam: Rodopi, 1998), p. 47.

2. Evans, *Whitehead and Philosophy*, p. 56.

3. C. Robert Mesle, *Process-Relational Philosophy: An Introduction to Alfred North Whithead* (West Conshohocken, PA: Templeton Press, 2008), p. 3.

4. Evans, *Whitehead and Philosophy*, p. 82.

5. John Dewey, *Democracy and Education* (New York: The Free Press, 1916), p. 100.

6. Vito Perrone, *A Letter to Teachers: Reflections on Schooling and the Art of Teaching* (San Francisco, CA: Jossey-Bass, 1991), p. 27.

7. Evans, *Whitehead and Philosophy*, p. 3.

8. Evans, *Whitehead and Philosophy*, p. 59.
9. Alfred North Whitehead, *Adventures of Ideas* (New York: The Free Press, 1933), p. 274.
10. Mesle, *Process-Relational Philosophy*, p. 13.
11. Alfred North Whitehead, *The Aims of Education and Other Essays* (New York: The Free Press, 1929), p. 36.
12. John Dewey, *Experience and Education* (New York: Touchstone, 1938), p. 46.
13. Evans, *Whitehead and Philosophy*, p. 10.
14. Mesle, *Process-Relational Philosophy*, p. 9.
15. Evans, *Whitehead and Philosophy*, p. 12.
16. Evans, *Whitehead and Philosophy*, p. 25.
17. Dewey, *Democracy and Education*, p. 10.
18. Jay Martin, *The Education of John Dewey: A Biography* (New York: Columbia University Press, 2002), p. 498.
19. Vito Perrone, *Lessons for New Teachers* (Boston: McGraw Hill, 2000), p. 37.
20. Paulo Freire, *Pedagogy of Freedom: Ethics, Democracy, and Civic Courage* (Lanham, MD: Rowman and Littlefield, 1998), pp. 90–91.
21. Hazrat Inayat Khan, *Sufi Teachings Book 3: The Art of Personality* (Commodius Vicus e-Publisher, 2012), Location 1409.
22. Whitehead, *The Aims of Education*, p. 30.
23. Khan, *Sufi Teachings Book 3*, Location 1385.
24. Whitehead, *The Aims of Education*, p. 32.
25. Khan, *Sufi Teachings Book 3*, Location 906.
26. Dewey, *Democracy and Education*, pp. 101–102.
27. Khan, *The Art of Personality*, Location 258.
28. Dewey, *Democracy and Education*, p. 17.
29. Khan, *The Art of Personality*, Location 2352.
30. Whitehead, *The Aims of Education*, p. 31.
31. Whitehead, *The Aims of Education*, p. 34.
32. Dewey, *Democracy and Education*, p. 160.
33. Whitehead, *The Aims of Education*, p. 37.
34. Martin, *The Education of John Dewey*, p. 7.
35. Martin, *The Education of John Dewey*, p. 6.
36. Khan, *Sufi Teachings Book 3*, Location 1385.
37. Dewey, *Experience and Education*, p. 46.
38. Whitehead, *The Aims of Education*, p. v.
39. Whitehead, *The Aims of Education*, p. 31.
40. Whitehead, *The Aims of Education*, p. 31.
41. Whitehead, *The Aims of Education*, p. 31.
42. Mesle, *Process-Relational Philosophy*, p. 30.
43. Dewey, *Experience and Education*, p. 48.
44. Evans, *Whitehead and Philosophy*, p. 99.
45. Perrone, *A Letter to Teachers*, p. 115.

46. Evans, *Whitehead and Philosophy*, p. 61.
47. Khan, *The Art of Personality*, Location 1536.
48. Mesle, *Process-Relational Philosophy*, p. 96.
49. Dewey, *Experience and Education*, p. 74.
50. Perrone, *A Letter to Teachers*, p. 27.
51. Dewey, *Experience and Education*, p. 61.
52. Whitehead, *The Aims of Education*, p. 53.
53. Hazrat Inayat Khan, *The Heart of Sufism: Essential Writings of Hazrat Inayat Khan* (Boston, MA: Shambhala, 1999), p. 179.
54. "Pittsburgh Here After Stormy Trip," *New York Times*, February 27, 1923, p. 21.
55. "Pittsburgh Here After Stormy Trip," *New York Times*, p. 21.
56. "American Women Victims of Hindu Mysticism." *Idaho Statesman*, February 18, 1912, p. 6.
57. "American Women Victims of Hindu Mysticism." *Idaho Statesman*, p. 6.
58. Hazrat Inayat Khan, *Sufi Teachings Book One: The Way of Illumination* (Commodius Vicus E-Publisher, 2012), Location 631.
59. Khan, *The Way of Illumination*, Location 632.
60. Whitehead, *The Aims of Education*, p. 29.
61. Whitehead, *The Aims of Education*, p. 29.
62. Whitehead, *The Aims of Education*, p. 37.
63. Whitehead, *The Aims of Education*, p. 32.
64. Whitehead, *Adventures of Ideas*, p. 47.
65. Whitehead, *The Aims of Education*, p. 1.
66. Evans, *Whitehead and Philosophy*, p. 45.
67. Malena Ernman, "Malena Ernman on Daughter Greta Thunberg: 'She was slowly disappearing into some kind of darkness'." *The Guardian*, February 23, 2020. Retrieved from https://www.theguardian.com/environment/2020/feb/23/great-thunberg-malena-ernman-our-house-is-on-fire-memoir-extract, February 26, 2020.
68. Ernman, "Malena Ernman on Daughter Greta Thunberg,"
69. Ernman, "Malena Ernman on Daughter Greta Thunberg,"
70. Ernman, "Malena Ernman on Daughter Greta Thunberg,"
71. Ernman, "Malena Ernman on Daughter Greta Thunberg,"
72. Khan, *The Heart of Sufism*, p. 209.
73. Jane Addams, *On Education* (London: Transaction Publishers, 2002), p. 57.

CHAPTER 6

"Well Done, Young Man"

Alfred North Whitehead not only provided us with the foundation for our educational philosophy, he also provided teachers with a powerful and practical framework with which we can put this philosophy into practice. One of the most attractive elements of Whitehead's framework is that, rather than being an imposition of an artificial ideal of what learning should be, it requires teachers to tap into and utilize the *natural* cycles of individual learning. Harold Dunkel notes that Whitehead sees "education as a process for which the student is naturally ready, not as one which is foreign to his nature."[1]

Evans notes that Whitehead's process philosophy is one of *organism*, a "worldview . . . based on processes associated with living things."[2] As discussed in the previous chapter, in our formulation children are alive, and are people. Whitehead argued that the failure of most educational theories and models lies in their being fundamentally *unnatural*. The failure, he wrote, "is because our tasks are set in an unnatural way, without rhythm."[3] He continued, "Lack of attention to the rhythm and character of mental growth is a main source of wooden futility in education."[4]

Thus, for Whitehead, the first step to developing a theory of education was to observe the process of learning, and find this natural rhythm. He believed, "theory based upon understanding of the nature of things [was] essential to a profession."[5] Based upon his observations and his trial and effort, Whitehead came to note, "Life is essentially periodic," and that within these periods of change were "cyclic recurrences."[6] He identified a three-cycle, recurring, periodic, rhythmic process of learning in which all humans engage, and with which he urged all educators to cooperate.

For Alfred North Whitehead, then, education was nothing less than a collaboration with nature. Whitehead called his framework the *rhythms of education*. Into these eddies of curiosity, building inexorably into currents of interest and learning, he believes we as teachers can find the mystical and sacred ground of education. Hyperbole? Whitehead wrote that the essence of education "is that it be religious," and he defined "religious education" as "an education which inculcates duty and reverence."[7]

Borrowing and then adapting Hegel, Whitehead describes these three stages of the learning process as *romance*, *precision*, and *generalization*. These stages correspond with the three components of our philosophy, *interest*, *humility*, and *wisdom*, respectively. Process philosophy's ultimate test, and the ultimate test of the theory of the naturally occurring rhythms of education, is to ask if we, as Whitehead argued we would, can observe these cyclic rhythms in action, confirming it through Dewey's cherished paradigm of experience.

Romance (Interest)

The kid knew better than to just stand there in front of the television like that. Were it not excruciatingly, unbearably hot outside, his Dad would have run him off for such an offense. "Please move from in front of the TV," he said, finding a sudden reserve of patience that surprised him.[8] But the kid didn't move, insistently asking more questions.

Dad wanted to support his eleven-year-old son's curiosity, but this was Jaws, and Jaws was his favorite movie. And Sheriff Brody and the boys were hurtling headlong towards their climactic confrontation with the Great White. No matter. His son, Hunter, was enthralled by the scene he had just watched and the Stephen King-worthy story of the USS Indianapolis.

"Is that story true?" Hunter demanded after actor Robert Shaw's chillingly morose performance as a survivor of the Indianapolis. Yes, Dad replied. "Tell me more about it!" Hunter practically begged.[9] An educator—school principal to be precise—his father answered the way any good educator might: "If you want to know more, I will take you to the library and you can check out a book on the USS Indianapolis."[10] And so it began.

For Alfred North Whitehead, the initial stage of romance was characterized by "novelty," "possibilities," and "wonder."[11] Evans is beautifully descriptive with the words he chooses to describe this first stage of learning: "interest," "encounter," "wonder," "imagination," "involvement," "zest," and "the dominant feeling should be joy."[12] During this phase, we seek to make the most of a young person's natural curiosity. Recall that Whitehead threw down the gauntlet for educators when he forcefully asserted there could be no learning without interest. He is not ambivalent or vague on this point, as we have seen.

Thus, this first step of the learning process requires that teachers take into account the personalities, cultures, and communities of students in order to better find approaches that will interest them. Let's be clear: Whitehead is not calling for students' interests and likes to drive our curriculum. He is arguing that we approach our curriculum and present it with an ever-observant eye toward who our students are. This admonition that interest must be present for learning to occur leads us to this first stage where we endeavor, by a clever and passionate approach to the topic, to pique the interest of our students and convince them that what we have to say is worth hearing.

It is here that we attempt to present the most appealing and intriguing facets of our subject to the students. In short, we get them to give us a chance. Recall Perrone's statement that teaching children is about *knowing* children. To know a child deeply enough that one has a sense of what approaches may best raise interest is the requirement for teachers in this initial stage of learning. It is a daunting, awesome demand that Whitehead's approach makes of us. It is also the surest approach to success in a classroom, in other words to teach *and* reach our students.

There are strategies—but no tricks—for getting to know our students well. The most important step is to *listen to them*. Take time every single day to speak with them about things beyond the curriculum. Ask about activities and hobbies, pay attention to their lives outside of the classroom, and then bring those interests in whenever possible. Take time to make the effort to connect what you are studying to their world. Make relevance as a purposeful goal. Supplement these conversations with surveys and questionnaires.

The system will make sure you know the numbers they believe defines your children; you must seek out the stories that actually do. Those test scores are significantly less useful to you than knowing their favorite movie, their favorite band/song, and their favorite (and most hated) sports teams. Does she play piano? Does he dance? Does she play volleyball? Is he in drama or choir? Madison Avenue might call this market research "knowing your audience." On this first stage, however, the other two depend, and so the effort is of the utmost importance.

Having come to know our students well—their inner selves and their abilities and needs—we design our teaching around this knowledge in a way that allows them freedom to search, to question, and ultimately to learn. In our modern way of thinking, this stage is where the teacher "hooks" the student and draws them into the lesson. To plan for this step, we need to think of what "romance" really means.

For Alfred North Whitehead, this stage of romance was

> a process of discovery, a process of becoming used to curious thoughts, of shaping questions, of seeking for answers, of devising new experiences, of noticing what happens as the result of new ventures. This general process is both natural and of absorbing interest.[13]

What are the characteristics of romance in our lives? When discussing this question with my pre-service teachers, I ask them to list these characteristics and I write them on the board. Some of the typical responses I get are that romance is:

- Hard work
- The unexpected
- Passionate
- Going above and beyond the normal or the mundane
    - Spontaneous
    - Intimate
    - Involves knowing someone well
    - Thoughtful
    - Being vulnerable

All these apply to the use of romance in our classrooms.

Romance will be hard work. This is because to remain romantic requires constant vigilance. I have no idea who first coined the analogy that love (or, in this case romance) was like a fire, but that person was a towering genius. There is no more apt analogy available to us. What happens to a fire if it is not constantly tended? It burns out. The same is true with romance. This is a powerful reason why Whitehead's theory will not be reduced to stagnation. If we begin our lessons with romance, we will constantly be seeking to show our students and remind ourselves that our subject matters, that our subject has relevance.

Whitehead simply refuses to allow us to assume mute obedience or passive attention from those young minds under our care and responsibility. He says, *Earn it. Deserve it.* This stance also ensures that we do not take our love for our subject for granted. Infusing our work with romance means that we will never assume that students will want to learn our subjects, we will never take for granted the fact that we have to "defend our honor" every single day. Because we cannot take these things for granted, we will work diligently to keep the fire burning and to reach our students. In social studies, my experience has been that a good approach to fulfilling the romance stage is through biography. Whether studying a particular era of history, a geographic region, or a culture, I have found that the ability to place a human face on the subject makes my teaching efforts more successful. The use of biography in the classroom provides me with the "hook" I am looking for with my students. It works well in others subjects too. Math teachers could begin their lesson on the Pythagorean theorem with a quick story about the imminently interesting cult that Pythagoras inspired and led.

Science teachers might introduce a lesson on astronomy by telling the macabre tale of Galileo's middle finger, the remains of which now float in a jar in Italy where you can visit and gawk at the heretical finger that once traced the stars. Whitehead writes,

> There is no comprehension apart from romance. It is my strong belief that the cause of so much failure in the past has been due to the lack of careful study of the due place of romance. Without the adventure of romance, at the best you get inert knowledge without initiative, and at the worst you get contempt of ideas—without knowledge.[14]

In Whitehead's framework a teacher will use romance as salesmanship—as a way to draw the students into the world of having ideas and acting upon them. Screen legend Charles Chaplin wrote in his autobiography:

> History was a record of wickedness and violence, a continual succession of regicides and kings murdering their wives, brothers and nephews; geography merely maps; poetry nothing more than exercising memory. Education bewildered me with knowledge and facts in which I was only mildly interested.
>
> If only someone had used salesmanship, had read a stimulating preface to each study that could have titillated my mind, infused me with fancy instead of facts, amused and intrigued me with the legerdemain of numbers, romanticized maps, given me a point of view about history and taught me the music of poetry, I might have become a scholar.[15]

Although the world is no doubt better off with Chaplin's brilliance being used in the arts, his refrain of "I might have become a scholar" is one that should haunt us.

What Chaplin is calling for here is the exact same thing Whitehead proposes: a vital role for romance in education. Providing that stimulating preface and the fancy of which Chaplin speaks is a teacher's job. Injecting and maintaining romance in our classrooms is hard work, but we must compete now, even more so than in Whitehead's day, with a society built on instant gratification and pleasure. If we do not attend to this step and make every effort to hook our students and capture their attention, we will not succeed as educators.

Precision (Humility)

His teacher, Mrs. Prevatte, made the suggestion that changed his life and, literally, American history. She urged Hunter to reach out personally to survivors of the USS Indianapolis for what had now become his sixth-grade history fair project at Ransom Middle School.[16] Hunter found a local Navy newspaper and placed an ad introducing himself and his project and asking for survivors to contact him. It was a long shot.

Then Maurice Bell answered. From Bell, Hunter received a directory of survivors' names; he sent requests for information to 154 survivors, of whom 83 responded.[17] While some men sent 'curt one-sentence answers . . . others sent . . . envelopes full of material, including multiple-page personal narratives they'd written out in longhand or typed up years before."[18]

Hunter's supportive parents traveled with him to meet survivors who were not only willing but eager to have someone hear their story. They had felt silenced and ignored for so very long. From these and other sources, Hunter began to put together the story of both the Indianapolis, her crew, and its captain, Charles McVay III. It was a story of betrayal, scapegoating, and injustice. Hunter was appalled and determined. The world needed to know.

Having gained our students' attention by clever approaches and the use of freedom of exploration and questioning, we now must undertake the heavy lifting of scholarship. Once we move forward from the romance stage, it is "time for pushing on, for knowing the subject exactly, and for retaining in the memory its salient features. This is the stage of precision," according to Whitehead.[19] This stage of his model is the one with which we are all familiar, because it is the stage traditional education has always stressed. "This stage," writes Whitehead, "is the sole stage of learning in the traditional scheme of education, either at school or university."[20]

The fact that traditional education is focused on this stage alone does not, in fact, mean that it is being done well. Whitehead tells us that an overemphasis on this stage can be dangerous, but also reminds us of its necessity. Whitehead writes, "The stage [of precision] is dominated by the inescapable fact that there are right ways and wrong ways, and definite truths to be known."[21]

Evans provides the following example:

The thrill of the wind and wave and the beauty of sails and hull on water are the romance. Learning to steer, trim, and tack, to control the craft and to harmonize with natural forces is the stage of precision.[22]

This is the stage at which students acquire the knowledge they will eventually be asked/allowed to use. A cellist must learn her scales before she can play solos.

Like romance, the stage of precision also demands that we know our students, our school community, and the greater community beyond our campus. Precision requires a deft touch, a compassionate approach, patience, and discipline. As our students acquire new knowledge, they also must integrate and synthesize this information, and this is a process that can be painful. Education often forces us to question cherished ideals, some of which may not hold up to scrutiny. Whitehead wrote, "Wherever there is a creed, there is a heretic round the corner or in his grave."[23] Creeds and dogma do not yield lightly or easily to truth; they never have.

The Scopes "monkey trial" is a disturbing reminder of what often happens when facts run into persistent, relentless superstition. Our students will filter all new knowledge through the prism of who they are and what they already "know." "The facts," Evans writes, "may be recognized as indisputable, but what they mean is open to interpretation because of past experience and the feelings associated with it."[24]

I traveled with a group of Cherokee High School students to Rome, Georgia, where my students did a presentation about their Cherokee history and culture for a group of eighth graders at Rome Middle School. We walked into the classroom, and one of my students noticed the large poster of Abraham Lincoln with the word *Honesty* emblazoned on it that was hanging prominently on the wall.

"He's also a murderer," she told the teacher, who was clearly startled. My student was no neo-confederate, though, and she proceeded to educate the teacher about the Dakota War of 1862 and the tragic execution of the Dakota 38. The Great Emancipator meant something very, very different to this Native American student than he did to the middle school teacher.

This does not mean that facts are negotiable in our classrooms. It does mean, though, that we must be prepared for the struggle of many students as they attempt to navigate their way through and to interpret what they are learning. We must humble ourselves and allow them to synthesize the material in their own way and at their pace. We may help them acquire knowledge but we cannot impose an interpretation on them. Perhaps, you are an admirer of President Lincoln. Perhaps you believe that, in the great balance of things, he did more good than bad and is worthy of being on a middle school wall. That is a valid argument.

So, of course, is the belief that the injustice of the Dakota 38 is enough to take him out of the "hero" ranks. Our job is to make certain that our students know how to find facts and that they have the intellectual and ethical disposition to interpret them honestly. It is not our job to interpret the facts for them. That is indoctrination. The stage of precision is not a passive stage; students should be actively engaged in this stage and not mute receptacles for the state's prepackaged curriculum.

The emphasis on precision should not be interpreted to mean that this stage is to be presented without reference to our students. Whitehead takes great pain to insist, "During the stage of precision, romance is the background . . . romance is not dead, and it is the art of teaching to foster it amidst definite application to appointed task."[25] We may have entered the stage of precision, but Whitehead wants us to keep the fires burning. So, the teacher must not follow romance with mind-numbing and painfully boring precision; we must strive to present this material in as pleasurable and, I dare say entertaining, a way as possible.

We keep the stage of precision interesting and infused with romance, he wrote,

> If the tasks correspond to the natural cravings of the pupil at his stage of progress, if they keep his powers at full stretch, and if they attain an obviously sensible result, and if reasonable freedom is allowed in the mode of execution.[26]

In our sought-after balance between freedom and discipline, this stage emphasizes discipline and is the vital bridge between the first and last stages. "The responsibility of the teacher at this stage is immense," Whitehead writes. "To speak the truth, except in the rare case of genius in the teacher, I do not think that it is possible to take a whole class very far along the road of precision without some dulling of interest."[27]

The precision stage will be a challenge because of its disciplined approach, and some students will long for more pure romance. But to skip this stage or to give it too little attention is to fail in our responsibilities as educators. In short, we want our students to think, yes. *But we must give them something about which to think*. Again, Whitehead stressed the need for discipline in this middle stage because, as he so forcefully phrased it, "there are right ways and wrong ways, and definite truths to be known."[28]

He also describes the function of this stage of learning as "the definite acquirement of allotted tasks."[29] Evans describes the stage of precision as being characterized by "discipline, mastery, and will" and points out that this is the moment when "new knowledge is added to the rudimentary information acquired during the stage of romance."[30]

There is a danger that comes with the stage of precision, a danger with which teachers in America deal daily. It is, after all, the precision stage alone with which standardized tests are concerned. Current notions of accountability in American education only take into account the accumulation of facts on the part of students. But to be effective, for genuine learning to occur, we cannot stop our model of teaching at this stage. It is not enough, for example, that a student knows that the Declaration of Independence was signed on July 4, 1776, or that it was written by Thomas Jefferson. This is the inert knowledge about which Whitehead warned us.

The important question is does the student understand the importance of the Declaration of Independence and how it affects his daily life? Is the student aware that young Chinese people died in Tienneman Square clutching Jefferson's words in the hope of one day knowing freedom? In Whitehead's model we must continue forward from the acquiring of facts to the using of facts; this is the stage Whitehead dubbed generalization.

Generalization (Wisdom)

There was a hush of surprised awe in the room when Admiral Donald Pilling, Vice Chief of Naval Operations, walked into the hearing room and sat at the table representing the United States Navy. It is September 14, 1999, and Hunter's dogged pursuit has led him here, before the Senate Armed Services Committee. From the stories he gathered and the documents he demanded Hunter stitched together the tragedy of Captain McVay, who had been wrongfully court-martialed over the sinking of the USS Indianapolis.

Understandably, the families of the sailors who had died demanded someone be held responsible for the horror and the tragedy. McVay was a third generation Navy man, and he knew how the game worked: "I think they're going to put it to me," he confided in resignation to a colleague.[31] He was right; the Navy's decision consigned him to a living hell for the next two decades. Though the survivors spoke against his court-martial and made efforts to clear their captain's name, the Navy stood coldly behind its decision. McVay was haunted—quite literally—by the tragedy.

His stepson recalled seeing him, weeping, clutching a letter of hate and vitriol he had received from a dead sailor's family. 'I can't take this,' he sobbed.[32] In November 1968 Charles McVay walked out of his house and into the yard, took out his pistol, and ended his life. Thirty years later, fourteen-year-old Hunter Scott, filled with righteous indignation and anger at the miscarriage of justice, had come to Congress to again plead for Captain McVay's legacy, memory, his family and those who remained of his crew. Behind him sat the veterans of the Indianapolis who had been able to travel.

Hunter lost the Florida state social studies competition on a technicality, a loss that devastated him. He came home from Tallahassee and hand-wrote letters to more than sixty survivors, apologizing for letting them down. Incredibly, they wrote him back. They thanked him for caring. They thanked him for trying. They assured him they were proud of him. And they urged him to never give up.

This morning his adversary was the second most powerful man in the United States Navy. Senate Armed Services Committee Chairman John Warner was also known to be very pro-Navy and seemed unlikely to rule against the wishes of Admiral Pilling. Hunter, though, was formidable. That interest first sparked by the scene from Jaws led to a search, a process of gathering and learning and synthesizing.

Now he had mastery of the story. The Navy saw a child; Hunter had become an expert. This became obvious as the hearing progressed, veering haphazardly off script and leaving Pilling and his staff scrambling to answer the piercing questions of the committee. Hunter, on the other hand, was ready with his answers, confident and quick. And accurate. As he concluded his testimony, he pulled out Captain McVay's dog tags, given to him by McVay's son. "I carry this as a reminder of my mission and in memory of the man who ended his own life in 1968. I carry this to remind me that only in the United States can one person make a difference, no matter what the age."[33]

When it was all over, Pilling appeared thunderstruck. The Navy lost; Hunter Scott won. More than fifty years after the tragedy, Captain Charles McVay III had his name cleared. Afterwards, Hunter approached Admiral Pilling. "Excuse me, sir," he said respectfully, "I'd like to give you a copy of my research, because it appeared you had some difficulty answering some of the questions, and I think this will provide you with some of the answers."[34] *The son who had given Hunter the dog tags told him he believed his father was "looking down" on him and his work and thinking, "Well done, young man."*[35]

Alfred North Whitehead states bluntly, "Knowledge does not keep any better than fish."[36] We have already seen that he defines the proper outcome of education as wisdom, and sees wisdom as the application and use of knowledge. His entire framework is a battle cry against his dreaded inert facts. To this point in his model the teacher has employed romance to gain her students' attention and care, and then assisted her students in the hard work of sorting and understanding and synthesizing certain, new, facts.

Now, in the final stage of Whitehead's rhythms, the students must again return, or cycle back, to a stance of freedom and apply the facts while constructing *their own* meaning from the material. Whitehead writes that

> something definite is now known; aptitudes have been acquired; and general rules and laws are clearly apprehended both in their formulation and their detailed exemplification. The pupil now wants to use his new weapons. He is an effective individual, and it is effects that he wants to produce . . . the stage of generalisations is the stage of shedding details in favor of the active application of principles, the details retreating into subconscious habits.[37]

The acquisition of knowledge is naturally followed by its use and application, a stage reduced to the insufficient word "assessment" in modern schools of education.

This stage of generalization is about ensuring that knowledge gained is knowledge employed (or, if you prefer, deployed). In this final stage, Whitehead requires the educator to allow her students to use the information they have acquired, and would certainly agree with James Allen's axiom, "Until thought is linked with purpose there is no intelligent accomplishment."[38]

This is the logical final step in an education. Seeing the natural cycle recurring, Whitehead notes of this stage, "There is here a reaction towards romance."[39] The freedom of use and the construction of values and opinions based on mastery of valid facts bring our student back to a place of novelty and enjoyment, and the rhythm starts again.

Generalization is the stage where true assessment can happen. If a child can translate material and put that material to work, then authentic learning has happened. One of the current buzz-phrases in education is "performance-based assessment," or "authentic assessment." Whitehead writes that "the essence of this stage is the emergence from the comparative passivity of being trained into the active freedom of application."[40] A better definition of education has not been postulated by anyone, anywhere. In a Whiteheadian model, the questions have more than one answer, are thoughtful and thought-provoking, are open-ended, and honor student opinions and voices as long as they are grounded in precision.

Bubble sheets do not lend themselves to wisdom. The stage of generalization asks students to make connections and find relationships across the curriculum and throughout society. Students are encouraged and empowered to wrestle with the material rather than swallow pre-made opinions and values. "An education which does not begin by evoking initiative and end by encouraging it," Whitehead wrote, "must be wrong."[41]

Initiative is encouraged by the active use of information and knowledge, or what Whitehead called wisdom. "Knowledge becomes wisdom," Malcolm D. Evans writes, "When its context is widened and connections are made that go beyond the immediate insistent facts. Wisdom requires [a] kind of synthesis or integration."[42]

In this model of the rhythms of education, the final product is a student capable of and interested in learning, in seeking and acknowledging relatedness, a student open to novelty and its integration. For our democratic society, the final result of such a model of teaching is Dewey's ideal too—a student progressing toward active, positive citizenship. We focus our pedagogy on the individual child, but our goals are, in the final analysis, for our world.

Such an ideal is, to be sure, at odds with our current system of education. Evans admits as much, writing,

> It is difficult in this age of accountability, objective assessment, etc., to think in terms of wisdom. Scores on the SAT, class rank, grades, results of standardized testing driving educational practice are paramount. The nature of knowledge acquired and its relationship to a life worth living is absent from our conversations.[43]

But children are not numbers; their lives must not be reduced to a test score or a percentile. It is past time we discard the wildly outdated industrial factory model of schooling. It has both failed and damaged enough generations.

Whitehead's philosophy is one of organism, and it stands in opposition to the mechanistic view that is prevalent in our culture. The rhythms of education model require educators to see our students as individuals with agency and emphasize the relatedness as well as the uniqueness of every child and young person we will have the honor to teach. Hazrat Inayat Khan wrote,

> The male and female, beast and bird, vegetable and rock, and all classes of things and beings are linked together and attracted to each other with a chord of harmony. *If one being or thing, however apparently useless, were missing in this universe of endless variety, it would be as it were a note missing in a song.* [Italics mine][44]

American education is more concerned in churning out a workforce than a citizenry. Chomsky points out,

> "What we have in place in the United States is not a system that encourages independent thought and critical thinking. On the contrary, our so-called democratic schools are based on an instrumental skills-banking approach that often prevents the development of the kind of thinking that enables one to "read the world" critically and to understand the reasons and linkages behind facts.[45]

Whitehead's model provides us with a desperately needed antidote for such a system.

Evans suggests the use of Whitehead's rhythms of education should lead to our replacing the machine as our symbol of education with one of the Tree of Life to reflect a new paradigm emphasizing growth, change, and organic processes that make up a true education. "Thinking of human beings in the same way as we think about machines," wrote Evans, "is so contrary to the nature of human beings, particularly as learners, that the current mechanistic context for modern society creates virtually insurmountable problems for educating in that society."[46]

If we hope to use the rhythms of education to overcome these systemic and cultural obstacles, we should first test the model. Whitehead claimed to have developed this framework based on his observations of learning; can we observe these rhythms for ourselves? Does Whitehead's claim that he is describing a naturally occurring cycle hold up to scrutiny? Throughout this chapter I have shared the inspiring story of Hunter Scott, the middle school student from Florida whose crusade on behalf of the survivors of the USS *Indianapolis* and their late captain, Charles McVay, rewrote a chapter of World War II history.

"As I listened to the story of men being attacked by sharks," he recalled later, "*I was fascinated*" [emphasis mine].[47] His interest ignited, Hunter dove into the facts, acquiring knowledge and perspective. He struggled to integrate his terrific disappointment in the Navy and the US government with his natural patriotism. He faced opposition from powerful institutions even though he clearly had the facts on his side. Many adults—including quite a few of the survivors themselves—told him to give up.

His dad—the school principal—told him to stick with it. "My dad says all young people need dream builders in their lives," sixteen-year-old Hunter recalled. "He says that too many students are surrounded by dream destroyers."[48] With such an ally, Hunter dug deeper and deeper and then used this new knowledge—beginning with letters to President Bill Clinton and Secretary of the Navy John Dalton. Neither responded favorably. Undeterred, Hunter continued until, eventually, he triumphed that day on Capitol Hill. *Romance*, *precision*, and *generalization*. Surely with the remarkable Hunter Scott we can agree these culminated in wisdom.

The incomparable activist Will D. Campbell believed the surest way to ruin a good thing was to give it respectability. Whitehead called his philosophical works "speculative philosophy," emphasizing the transitory nature of knowledge and his inherent contempt for and suspicion of dogma. His rhythms of education framework, therefore, can and should be manipulated, experimented with, and adapted to the circumstances of the school, the community, and of course the individual teachers and students.

Speaking of the different revolutions that had shaped and reshaped our world, Whitehead observed, "The solution was merely temporary, and so is the planet itself."[49] The rhythms can be translated as lesson plans. Teachers have told me about planning their week by using Whitehead's paradigm. Organizing units on this basis has also been a successful approach. It is important to remember that you are not imposing this model on your students, you are tapping into their own natural rhythms of learning. The outcome for which we strive, wisdom, is extraordinarily ambitious.

"Wisdom," Hazrat Inayat Khan wrote, "is greater and more difficult to attain than intellect, piety, or spirituality."[50] Yet we know we live in uncertain and, often, frightening times. We face existential threats unthinkable to previous generations and, as such, we require new approaches and patterns. Merely well-informed men—in Whitehead's acidic phrase—have gotten us here to a dying planet and wealth inequality like the world has never known. We are educating for a world that no longer exists.

The acceptance of the transmission of inert ideas—his slur for "ideas that are merely received into the mind without being utilised, or tested, or thrown into fresh combinations"—has led us to this place where a "war on facts" and a "war on truth" can thrive.[51] Alfred North Whitehead's rhythms of education offer teachers the chance to educate for life and for living, to empower the young in our care to become the citizens and the leaders we need them to be and which they were, in fact, born to be.

Notes

1. Harold B. Dunkel, *Whitehead on Education* (Columbus, OH: Ohio State University Press, 1965), p. 85.
2. Evans, *Whitehead and Philosophy of Education*, p. 21.
3. Alfred North Whitehead, *The Aims of Education and Other Essays* (New York: The Free Press, 1929), p. 20.
4. Whitehead, *Aims of Education*, p. 17.
5. Alfred North Whitehead, *Adventures of Ideas* (New York: The Free Press, 1933), p. 57.
6. Whitehead, *Aims of Education*, p. 17.
7. Whitehead, *Aims of Education*, p. 14.
8. Pete Nelson, *Left for Dead: A Young Man's Search for Justice for the USS Indianapolis* (New York: Delacorte Press, 2002), p. xii.
9. Nelson, *Left for Dead*, p. xii.
10. Nelson, *Left for Dead*, p. xiii.
11. Whitehead, *Aims of Education*, pp. 17; 32.
12. Evans, *Whitehead and Philosophy of Education*, p. 1.
13. Whitehead, *Aims of Education*, p. 32.
14. Whitehead, *Aims of Education*, p. 33.
15. Charles Chaplin, *My Autobiography* (New York: Simon and Schuster, 1964), p. 41.
16. Nelson, *Left for Dead*, p. 12.
17. Nelson, *Left for Dead*, p. 151.
18. Nelson, *Left for Dead*, p. 151.
19. Whitehead, *Aims of Education*, p. 34.
20. Whitehead, *Aims of Education*, p. 34.

21. Whitehead, *Aims of Education*, p. 34.
22. Evans, *Whitehead and Philosophy of Education*, p. 31.
23. Whitehead, *Adventures of Ideas*, p. 52.
24. Evans, *Whitehead and Philosophy of Education*, p. 92.
25. Whitehead, *Aims of Education*, p. 34.
26. Whitehead, *Aims of Education*, p. 35.
27. Whitehead, *Aims of Education*, p. 35.
28. Whitehead, *Aims of Education*, p. 34.
29. Whitehead, *Aims of Education*, p. 35.
30. Evans, *Whitehead and Philosophy of Education*, p. 31.
31. Doug Stanton, *In Harm's Way: The Sinking of the USS Indianapolis and the Extraordinary Story of Its Survivors* (New York: Saint Martin's Paperbacks, 2001), p. 247.
32. Stanton, *In Harm's Way*, p. 261.
33. Nelson, *Left for Dead*, p. 170.
34. Nelson, *Left for Dead*, p. 184.
35. Nelson, *Left for Dead*, p. xviii.
36. Whitehead, *Aims of Education*, p. 98.
37. Whitehead, *Aims of Education*, pp. 36–37.
38. James Allen, *As a Man Thinketh* (Public Domain), p. 35.
39. Whitehead, *Aims of Education*, p. 36.
40. Whitehead, *Aims of Education*, p. 37.
41. Whitehead, *Aims of Education*, p. 37.
42. Evans, *Whitehead and Philosophy of Education*, p. 76.
43. Evans, *Whitehead and Philosophy of Education*, p. 77.
44. Hazrat Inayat Khan, *Sufi Teachings Book 2: The Mysticism of Music, Sound and Word* (Commodius Vicus, E-Publisher, 2012), Location 344 Kindle edition.
45. Noam Chomsky, *Chomsky on Miseducation*, Donaldo Macedo, Ed. (Lanham, MD: Rowman and Littlefield Publishers, 2000), p. 3.
46. Evans, *Whitehead and Philosophy of Education*, p. 20.
47. Nelson, *Left for Dead*, p. xii.
48. Nelson, *Left for Dead*, p. xv.
49. Whitehead, *Adventures of Ideas*, p. 46.
50. Hazrat Inayat Khan, *Sufi Teachings Book 5: Spiritual Liberty* (Commodius Vicus, E-Publisher, 2012), Location 517 Kindle edition.
51. Whitehead, *Aims of Education*, p. 1.

CHAPTER 7

Dispatch from the Jericho Road

Only in America could mass delusion steeped in ethnocentrism and superstition be labeled a "great awakening," but this nation had two of them. To be fair, the fever was not confined to the United States. In 1806, Ms. Mary Bateman, known to posterity as the "Yorkshire Witch," had glommed onto a group of desperate seekers in Leeds, called Southcottians, after the charismatic evangelist they followed. Bateman, born in 1768 to a family of poor, small farmers, had displayed "a knavish and vicious disposition" from early in life.[1]

In her late thirties at the time of her activities in Leeds, Mary Bateman was a thief, a fraud, and an all-around charlatan. Her most infamous religious con was a miracle hen which laid eggs emblazoned with the Southcottian motto, "Christ is Coming." The faithful of Leeds, awed by the supernatural wonder, happily paid a shilling each to see the miracle eggs of Leeds. The desire of these gullible followers to believe is captured by Bateman's biographer.

> "Persons . . . flocked from all quarters to see the wonderful egg, and they who dared to disbelieve, and to insinuate that some fraud had been practiced, stood as good a chance of being maltreated by a credulous multitude, as he who in Italy should venture to question the reality of the miracles wrought by the thumb of *Thomas the Apostle*, or he who in Spain should be so foolhardy as not to fall down and prostrate himself before the miraculous works of the Lady of the Pillar!"[2] *They who dared to disbelieve. . . .* The pilgrims wanted so badly to believe.

We mustn't pick on our nineteenth-century friends, though. By 2019, hundreds of pilgrims had traveled to the small town of Dalton, Georgia, to be inspired or perhaps even healed by the local miracle—a Bible that mysteriously oozed what was believed to be a supernatural oil. There were those who traveled for hours every week to view the Bible or to replenish their vials of miracle oil (more than 400 gallons of which had been oozed by January 2020), and there were even more dedicated believers who moved to Dalton to be closer to the Bible, which was owned by a local man named Jerry Pearce.[3]

A reporter noted, "Believers say the translucent oil has cured skin conditions and cancer. They say it has generated crystals, changed color, and increased in volume. . . . They say small vials of oil refilled themselves overnight."[4] The oil was even able to affect geopolitical miracles, with one woman reporting that she had given some to a friend who had taken it with him to North Korea, where he "slathered three rocks there with oil . . . 'Right after that was when Trump met with Kim Jong-un,' she said. The crowd murmured in awe."[5] The miracle was, sadly, too good to be true.

A *Chattanooga Times Free Press* reporter, some chemical analysis from researchers at the University of Tennessee-Chattanooga, and a couple of eyewitnesses from a Tractor Supply store all combined to unravel the tale of the miracle Bible and its healing oil. Some believers were, however, undeterred. Leah Lesesne was one who frankly told a reporter that

> she wasn't sure how much she cared whether the oil Bible was real. 'It has brought people closer to God, it has brought people healing, it has rekindled people's faith and curiosity. . . . Even if one day it's proven that all this was a sham.'[6]

Even if all this was a sham. The pilgrims, it seems, still want so badly to believe.

From Copernicus to Galileo to John Scopes, scholars have often been despised and rejected for the inconvenient truths we preach. The credulous pilgrims of Leeds and Dalton are hardly extraordinary in their stubborn desire to cling to their hopes and beliefs. In that stance, they are all too human. For teachers, this means we are often cast in the role of bearers of bad news, the ones who require our students to question certain things their parents or the community (or both) may not *want* to be questioned. Educators are often the ones left with the responsibility of pointing out that the emperor is wearing no clothes.

This is a perilous place to be—a professional, ethical, and moral high-wire act. It is for this reason that this is not a chapter that will argue that new teachers—or even veteran teachers—should be unafraid. There is, in fact, plenty about which we can and should be afraid. As Carl Sagan memorably wrote, "Those who are not afraid of monsters tend not to leave descendants."[7] The subtitle to Dana Goldstein's book *The Teacher Wars* aptly calls teaching as "America's most embattled profession." This has historically been the case, but the vitriol has never, it seems, been so great or the stakes so very high.

In this age of instant outrage and cancel culture, in a time when righteous indignation far outpaces righteousness, the attacks on teaching and teachers are particularly ugly and come from all sides of the political spectrum. Hypocrisy, after all, has always been bipartisan. Buffeted by these warring factions, competing ideologies, and a dedicated crew of wingnuts committed to ending public education entirely, teachers are left anxious, emotionally battered, and exhausted. While not apolitical, most educators got into the profession for humanistic, not political, reasons.

Still, here we are, and with this reality teachers need ways to mitigate this fear—to prepare for it, confront it, and keep it in check. I am going to offer four approaches for dealing with the fear with which many new teachers struggle. First, we need to remind ourselves that we need not be fearless in order to succeed and maintain sanity. Second, we should understand that often the role of an educator is to be a troublemaker—to take on sacred tales and beliefs. Third, a teacher keeps fear in check by relentless self-assessment, making sure we are all about *good* trouble. Finally, to lessen the troubles that lead to our fears, teachers must know the material they teach fully and deeply.

The first step in our fight against fear is to remind ourselves that we need not be fearless in order to be courageous. Sacheen Littlefeather was extremely scared when, on March 27, 1973, she made her voice heard in protest of Hollywood's longstanding abysmal treatment and portrayal of American Indians. She had just begun her speech announcing Marlon Brando's refusal to accept his award for *The Godfather*, when, "some of those in attendance began to growl," in the words of one account.[8] "The rising rumble clearly unnerved Littlefeather," this description continued, "who lost her way for a moment."[9]

> But only for a moment. She recovered and made her statement . . . and paid a price. In the immediate aftermath she had to be protected from John Wayne. Though the Duke had not been willing to fight Nazis, he was willing to go after the physically diminutive Littlefeather, and had to be restrained by six security guards. In the bigger picture, she found herself blacklisted. She remembered, "the government was madder than hell. Afterward they came looking for me, and told everyone in the studios in Hollywood not to hire me."[10]

Looking back decades later, though, Littlefeather could laugh, "Me and the Creator are OK."[11] Littlefeather's momentary fear is hardly recalled; but many remember her quiet dignity and her ferocious determination to be heard on behalf of herself and her people. Courageous and fearless are not the same—to be truly fearless would be a foolish effort to turn off hard-wired (and life-saving) biology. Educators need not be fearless, but we must be courageous; courageous enough to teach truth to power when necessary.

Parker Palmer has dedicated an entire book to the need for courage in education. Teaching, he points out, "is always done at the dangerous intersection of personal and public life," a reality that places teachers on highly charged and contentious ground.[12] The very nature of the work can breed fear. My favorite book on teaching is Stuart B. Palonsky's *900 Shows a Year*, and in it he recounts a moment of distinct near-terror from his first year of teaching. It was an assembly for five hundred students that was supervised by "about fifteen teachers."[13]

A veteran teacher realized the presentation on career choices was going to end short of the end-of-day bell. "Spread the word," the teacher told Palonsky with a military air and a touch of foreboding.[14] As predicted, the lights came up and the students herded for the exits. Palonsky found himself the only thing standing between a mass of students and freedom. He told them—rather apologetically—that they would have to wait for the bell. "I was uncomfortable," he remembered, "unsure of my ability to control the students."[15] In addition to fears about control and discipline, Palmer notes the fear that exists for educators even when a lesson is a rousing success and inspires spirited debate and discussion.

"If we embrace diversity," he writes, "we find ourselves on the doorstep of our next fear: fear of the conflict that will ensue when divergent truths meet."[16] We can fill volumes with the myriad fears that can and will haunt a teacher from time to time. But fear, it turns out, is baked in to the human condition and experience. That is a feature, not a failure, of humanity. Let stuntmen and women be fearless; teachers succeed when they are courageous.

Our second approach to taming fear is to, within reason and common sense, embrace the natural role of teacher as troublemaker. Many teachers carry fear into their classrooms because, somewhere down deep, they understand that being a truly effective educator means causing a little trouble from time to time. There is, in fact, something necessarily iconoclastic about education. Most sacred cows don't withstand close scrutiny. North Dakota students attending a high school remodeled and refurbished with funds pouring in from the Bakken oil fields may not want to hear that fossil fuels are driving the death of the planet. That does not, however, make the fact less of a fact.

It turns out that facts, like God, are no respecter of persons. Teaching and teachers have never stood aloof from the cultural and political winds, but never before has the profession been under such constant assault from within and without. As our politics have become ever more toxic and divided and our culture more fractured, teaching has been both pawn and victim. Howard Zinn argued that not only could teachers not avoid controversy, we should not *want* to do so.

In his essay "The Uses of Scholarship," Zinn calls the notion of teacher neutrality, "a disservice to the very ideals we teach about as history, and a betrayal of the victims of an unneutral world."[17] He also points out the danger of such scholarship, writing, "The call [for neutrality] is naïve, because there are powerful interests already at work in the academy, with varying degrees of self-consciousness."[18] Freire labels a teacher's attempted neutrality as "a comfortable and perhaps hypocritical way of avoiding any choice or even hiding my fear of denouncing injustice."[19]

Embracing our inner troublemaker has never been more essential to the teacher's role within the maintenance and transmission of our democratic ideals. Frankly, educators have been too willing to coddle ignorance, bigotry, and superstition, and our nation is paying a horrifically high price. A combination of toxic culture, feckless administrators, and well-connected ideologues have left teachers exposed and understandably hesitant to confront controversial issues within our classroom, and our students' education, and, therefore our society, is the less for it.

Even before the phrase "alternative facts" had been uttered, an article in *Scientific American* warned that Americans were using "political orientation and ideology" rather than science to arrive at their opinions and beliefs.[20] That may be why in 2019 far fewer Americans believed that human activity caused climate change (29 percent)[21] than believed in ghosts (45 percent).[22] Teaching our students to be critical thinkers is of the utmost importance, and we should boldly proclaim, as did Clarence Darrow at the trial of John Scopes, "We have the purpose of preventing bigots and ignoramuses from controlling the education of the United States."[23]

While we should choose to embrace our role as troublemaker, we must also make sure we are about *good trouble*. This powerful "mischievous phrase" comes to us from the late civil rights legend and Georgia congressman John Lewis, and is our third way to confront fear.[24] Long before it became a popular hashtag, the ideal of causing good trouble was the foundation of Lewis's life and work. In 2015, Lewis gave the commencement address at Lawrence

University in Wisconsin, where he remembered his childhood of segregation and his questions to his family about the injustices by which they were surrounded.

The venerable congressman also remembered the timidity of the answers he received from his friends and relatives, all of whom urged him to ignore the bigotry and not cause any friction. As commencement speaker, Lewis instead urged his listeners to "find a way to get in the way."[25] In case any of the graduates missed the point, Lewis continued, "History will not be kind to us. So you have a moral obligation, a mission and a mandate, to speak up, speak out and get in good trouble."[26] For a teacher, *good trouble* is educating and teaching from a place of determined kindness and compassion.

A few things to be said here:

- The earth is not 6,000 years old
- Thomas Jefferson was a slave owner
- Creationism is superstition, not science, and has no place in a classroom
- Climate change is real and occurring all around us

The statements above are of facts, not opinions, and yet all are controversial, embattled, and might be avoided by new teachers hoping to stay out of the clutches of the Right or the Left. Perhaps more to the point, the pushback against these facts comes from the murky realm of belief—that island of safe certainty circled by the sharks of inconvenient truths.

When our cherished beliefs stand up to inspection, it provides a feeling of immense satisfaction and perhaps pride. Beliefs, when confirmed, can be a powerful vindication of heritage and culture. However, when our stories and beliefs fail to withstand closer scrutiny, it can be a dizzying experience that leaves students disoriented, confused, and, often, angry. For some, the difference between 6,000 and over 4 billion years old isn't just new information to be synthesized, it is sacrilege. Suddenly, the teacher is a threat.

The student who has been taught the romantic version of President Barack Obama—the intellectual, cool, avatar of progressivism—may struggle to reconcile the fact that Obama was responsible for unleashing three bombs an hour, every hour, every day, on civilians and combatants alike, during his final year in office.[27] Fans of Jefferson as the "Sage of Monticello" may not want to acknowledge the human bondage that provided the foundation of his existence, but Sally Hemings and the nameless others owned as property by the third president cry out for the justice of history. The Daughters of the Revolution are almost certain to raise a hue and cry, however.

An underappreciated aspect of teaching is just how uncomfortable true education is. Teachers fail to acknowledge this pain at their own peril. While we must teach uncomfortable truths, we should do so from a place of humility and kindness. Those who take perverse pleasure in these difficult moments are sadists, not educators. Good trouble means we never seek conflict or controversy, and that we understand and take seriously the emotional and psychological health of our students. Good trouble means being a fellow traveler, not a know-it-all oracle.

Turning back to Inayat Khan for a moment, he wrote of the painful process of learning:

> When [the student] strengthens his belief by knowledge then comes disbelief in things that his knowledge cannot cope with, and in things that he once believed in. An unbeliever is one who has changed his belief to disbelief; disbelief often darkens the soul, but sometimes it illuminates it.[28]

As any teacher can tell you, new knowledge that does not conform to prior beliefs often darkens the soul *as* it illuminates.

There will always be those, though, who desperately try to ignore the light. Khan writes,

> Sometimes belief proves to be worse than disbelief. This is when a person, set in his belief, hinders his own progress not allowing his mind to go further into the research of life, refusing guidance and advice from another, in order that he may preserve his own belief.[29]

I'd rather not know remains a powerful mantra for far too many of our fellow citizens, and that is a stance education must seek to demolish and scatter to the winds.

John Lewis's *good trouble* sought to destroy the evil of segregation, so it would be a terrible mistake to view the call for good trouble in our classrooms to be a call for passivity or strategic silences. Hardly. But we must remember that our students need and deserve kindness and compassion and patience as we ask them, over time, to put away childish things.

Our final approach for a teacher to fight fear is to master content. In short, *know your stuff*. Be more than incredulous—be paranoid about your sources and check them all again and again, especially the textbooks given to you by the state. James W. Loewen writes that history textbooks in America are so poor, "the more [history] courses students take, the stupider they become."[30] As educators we can best model scholarship for students by practicing it ourselves. We should look under, around, and from every angle at every "fact" we dare teach and take nothing for granted.

Nothing is sacred—question everything before you present it to the young and impressionable minds in your care and whose best interests are your responsibility. Find the other side. Take the story of Jay Silverheels as an example. In the pantheon of American Indian heroes Silverheels's name is conspicuously absent. Born Harold J. Smith in 1912 at Six Nations reserve, one of eleven children, Silverheels was an American Indian actor best known for his portrayal of Tonto, the side-kick to Clayton Moore's *Lone Ranger*.[31]

In the years that have ensued since the heyday of the *Lone Ranger* television show in the 1950s, Silverheels has come to symbolize for many activists and educators all that was and is wrong about Hollywood's treatment of the American Indian. The character Silverheels embodied is now mocked for his stilted delivery of lines that smack of pidgin English and belittled for his second banana status to a white vigilante of the Old West.

Silverheels (as the character Tonto) receives a thoroughly negative appraisal in Vine Deloria Jr.'s seminal work *Custer Died For Your Sins: An Indian Manifesto*. Deloria writes,

> The supreme archetype of the white Indian was born one day in the pulp magazines. This figure would not only dominate the pattern of what Indians had been and would be, but also actually block efforts to bring into focus the crises being suffered by Indian tribes.[32]

In Deloria's eyes, Silverheels almost single-handedly foisted a stereotype of American Indians on the world in which the Indian was "a little slower, a little dumber, had much less vocabulary, and rode a darker horse."[33] Deloria compares the character of Tonto with other "turncoats of history" such as Squanto and Keokuk.[34] His discussion of Tonto includes this passage:

> But Tonto never rebelled, never questioned the Lone Ranger's judgment, never longed to go back to the tribe for the annual Sun Dance. Tonto was a cultureless Indian for Indians and an uncultured Indian for whites.
>
> Tonto cemented in the minds of the American public the cherished falsehood that all Indians were basically the same—friendly and stupid.[35]

Silverheels's portrayal of Tonto was not the archetype of Hollywood at all, however—in fact, the character of Tonto was groundbreaking at the time and broke the mold of previous film and television representations of the American Indian.

Before Tonto, when a white audience saw an Indian come riding over the hill toward their hero, it meant only trouble. Films need villains, and for Hollywood the American Indian and the gangster filled those roles for decades. Tonto was one of the first film images of an American Indian who was a *good guy*; he was an American Indian who was bringing help, not coming to pillage the town and take advantage of the women folk. *The New York Times* made note of Silverheels's legacy, pointing out he "appeared in 85 films, usually portraying an American Indian at a time when it was rare for an Indian actor to do so."[36]

Tonto may not have helped discover Alcatraz Island, but he did force white Americans to take a new look at an American Indian as a loyal and brave force, not as merely the whooping natives swarming over the ridge to attack a wagon train. This fact alone could place Silverheels in that pantheon of American Indian greats to say nothing of his later years. Silverheels was determined to bring a touch of dignity, empathy, and pathos to his portrayal of Tonto, though he was under no illusions about what he was struggling against. "He's stupid," Silverheels lamented in 1957 about the character that had rocketed him to fame. "The Lone Ranger treats him like some kind of servant, and this seems to suit Tonto fine."[37]

In the 1960s, Jay Silverheels used his success to found the Indian Actors Workshop in Hollywood in an effort to support Native artists and as part of his continuing efforts to change the way American Indians appeared on film and TV screens, and he was the first American Indian to receive a star on Hollywood's Walk of Fame.[38] He also deployed a brutal and subversive sense of humor at times, using his Mohawk language to mock Hollywood. "I used to get a kick out of Harry speaking Mohawk," one friend recalled, "especially when it didn't go with the story line. Us Mohawk would be sitting in the Brantford movie house laughing, and all the other people would be wondering what was so funny."[39]

So, who was Silverheels, and what does he represent? Is he a tragic example of Littlefeather's complaints against Hollywood? Is he a trailblazer fighting for the same things for which Littlefeather fought? Was he a bit of both? Neither? Like virtually every other topic a teacher might discuss, there is something in the work of Silverheels and the character of Tonto to anger or offend folks from the Left and the Right. The deeper our knowledge of our subjects, the better prepared we may be when the slings and arrows of complaint come our way.

Teacher preparation programs do a catastrophically bad job with *content*—the heart of every teacher's existence. So much time is devoted to mindless and sophistic "technique" and attempting to annihilate whatever creativity and individualism our future teachers bring to the classroom that very little time is left for learning the actual content of what will be taught. For the time being this means that teachers are forced into the position of educating themselves about content once they've graduated and are beyond the busywork of their programs. This lack of content mastery (or even comfort) leaves new teachers reliant upon their textbooks, which are notoriously poor in terms of scholarship.

In order, therefore, for teachers to "know their stuff" enough to mitigate their fears, new teachers must commit wholeheartedly to being a lifelong learner. Yes, this phrase has become another hackneyed cliché of the profession, but it is a phrase that captures the essence of this challenge. A teacher must be a voracious reader and must possess an inquisitive and suspicious mind.

There will always be new things to learn, new perspectives to consider, and teachers must seek these out. It may not be possible to become an expert in every subject taught—think of elementary school teachers who are already expected to master the content of kindergarten through fifth or sixth grade—but that cannot serve as an excuse for not putting forth the effort to know as much as we can about everything we teach.

Knowing this content is not merely best practice, it is also an insurance against the angry parent who wants to know where you got your information about Abraham Lincoln and the Dakota 38. Having never been taught this information, Dad has a knee-jerk response to your diminishing Honest Abe in the eyes of his child. Dad shows up to school as angry as a primetime Fox News anchor, demanding answers. You pull out your dog-eared copy of David A. Nichols's *Lincoln and the Indians: Civil War Policy and Politics*, even offering to let Dad borrow the book and evaluate the scholarship for himself. Maybe Dad takes the book home; maybe not. Perhaps he is appeased; perhaps not. The teacher, however, has done her job and done it well.

∞

"Hey," the shaken father said, looking at his children across the table in the diner, "Look at me." His children, a thirteen-year-old son and ten-year-old daughter, had been staring at their pancakes with a mix of embarrassment and fright. They lifted their eyes to their father, who had been on the receiving-end of the stranger's furious tirade. "Doing the right thing," he told his children, "is not always popular. Some people will get mad at you."[40]

G. T. Bynum loved the food at Phill's Diner in Tulsa, but on this Sunday morning he got more than he bargained for as he sat with his family enjoying breakfast. The forty-two-year-old Bynum, mayor of Tulsa, was used to constituents approaching him wherever he went, but this exchange was different. The woman who approached his booth was livid, accusing the mayor of "doing this to make white people feel bad" and angrily ranting about "the blacks."[41] The "this" of which the woman spoke with such vitriol was Bynum's support for an examination of two sites in Tulsa that researchers believe are mass graves holding the remains of the victims of Tulsa's 1921 race riot and massacre.

"Geophysical scanning" done by researchers from the University of Oklahoma "identified two spots at the Oaklawn Cemetery that might bear bodies of those killed" in the Tulsa horror, and soon city leaders were confronted with the question of what to do with this information.[42] For Mayor Bynum, the question was not difficult—"It is very important for us to continue this search," he told one group of Tulsans, and speaking of the victims he said, "If they are there, we are going to find them."[43] Almost defiantly, Bynum has said, "We will follow the truth where that takes us."[44] Thanks in part to Bynum's courage, next year—the hundredth anniversary of the massacre—the riot will be taught in Oklahoma public schools. For the first time ever.[45]

The reality of the event is not at issue (no one has called the Tulsa massacre "fake news" yet), but the crazed woman at the diner was not alone in preferring to leave the past alone and let the story die. In 1921, of the hundreds of African Americans murdered, only thirty-five were "confirmed and identified."[46] The others—the *hundreds* of others—were buried in the unmarked, mass graves and lost to history.

Mayor Bynum's promise to locate them is not merely a historical wrong made right, it is a moral one. "The authorities never told [the survivors] where the bodies were ultimately buried"; reporter Vanessa Romo wrote, "There were never any funerals. There were no goodbyes from family members and no preachers offering prayers or words of comfort."[47] Even in the face of such injustice, however, not everyone in Phill's Diner was moved to supporting Bynum's efforts.

It is reasonable to fear such confrontation. It is reasonable to want to avoid such discomfort as much as possible. "Usually," Bynum said,

> My M.O. in a situation like that is to listen to the person and let them vent . . . [but after] five or six minutes, I felt I had to interject and point out the history of what happened.[48]

With the diner's other customers looking on awkwardly, Bynum "said he would not back down from trying to find answers."[49]

Ralph Waldo Emerson wrote that a scholar must, by definition, be both free and brave. "Brave," he wrote, "for fear is a thing which a scholar by his very function puts behind him. Fear," Emerson concludes, "always springs from ignorance."[50] Educators must be brave because, as we have all seen, ignorance will defend itself. On the last night of his life, Dr. Martin Luther King Jr. gave a speech in Memphis, Tennessee.

As a thunderstorm howled outside, Dr. King turned to the story of the Good Samaritan. "You remember," he told the gathered audience "that a Levite and a priest passed by" without helping the traveler who "fell among thieves" on the Jericho Road.[51] King ruminates over how, over two millennia, Christians have speculated about their motive—"we use our imagination to try to determine why the priest and the Levite didn't stop."[52]

There have been many theories—they were in a hurry; they lacked compassion; they lacked empathy and kindness; they were selfish. King, though, had a very different idea. "I'm going to tell you what my imagination tells me," he told his audience in the final sermon of his life. "It's possible that these men were afraid. You see, the Jericho road is a dangerous road."[53] Dr. King continued:

> In the days of Jesus it came to be known as the "Bloody Pass." And you know, it's possible that the priest and the Levite looked over that man on the ground and wondered if the robbers were still around. Or it's possible that they felt that the man on the ground was merely faking. And he was acting like he had been robbed and hurt, in order to seize them over there, lure them there for quick and easy seizure. And so the first question that the Levite asked was, "If I stop to help this man, what will happen to me?" But then the Good Samaritan came by. And he reversed the question: "If I do not stop to help this man, what will happen to him?"[54]

The "Good Samaritan" was also the *courageous* Samaritan. Dr. King points out that the fear of the priest and the Levite were not mere paranoia. The road to Jericho *was* treacherous and they had reason to be afraid. The Samaritan, though, overcame his fear. Dr. King posits the essential question we, too, must ask: "If I do not stop to help this man, what will happen to him?" For teachers the question more accurately is, "If I do not stop to help this student, what will happen to her?" Will she reject science and endanger her children? Will he ignore facts to be manipulated by a demagogue? Such outcomes—*risks*—are unacceptable. We must summon our courage and do our job.

Notes

1. N.A., *Extraordinary Life and Character of Mary Bateman, the Yorskshire Witch, Twelfth Edition* (Leeds: Davies and Company, 1811), p. 5.

2. N.A., *Extraordinary Life and Character of Mary Bateman*, p. 14.

3. Ruth Graham, "The Bible that Oozed Oil: A Small Georgia Town, a Prophecy about Donald Trump, and the Story of How a Miracle Fell Apart." *Slate*, February 27, 2020. Retrieved from https://slate.com/human-interest/2020/02/oil-bible-dalton-georgia-trump-prophecy-evangelical-miracle.html, March 19, 2020.

4. Graham, "The Bible that Oozed Oil."

5. Graham, "The Bible that Oozed Oil."

6. Graham, "The Bible that Oozed Oil."

7. Carl Sagan, *The Demon-Haunted World: Science as a Candle in the Dark* (New York: Ballantine Books, 1996), Location 1823, Kindle edition.

8. William J. Mann, "How Marlon Brando Made Hollywood Face Its Racism—at the Oscars." *The Daily Beast*, December 15, 2019. Retrieved from https://www.thedailybeast.com/how-marlon-brando-made-hollywood-face-its-racism-at-the-oscars, March 22, 2020.

9. Mann, "How Marlon Brando Made Hollywood face Its Racism."

10. Dexter Thomas, "Q&A: Meet the Woman Who Refused Marlon Brando's Oscar and Inspired Jada Pinkett Smith's Boycott." *Los Angeles Times*, February 5, 2016. Retrieved from https://www.latimes.com/entertainment/movies/moviesnow/la-et-mn-sacheen-littlefeather-oscars-20160204-htmlstory.html, March 22, 2020.

11. Thomas, "Q&A: Meet the Woman Who Refused Marlon Brando's Oscar."

12. Parker J. Palmer, *The Courage to Teach: Exploring the Inner Landscape of a Teacher's Life* (San Francisco, CA: Jossey-Bass, 1998), p. 17.

13. Stuart B. Palonsky, *900 Shows a Year: A Look at Teaching from a Teacher's Side of the Desk* (New York: Random House, 1986), p. 116.

14. Palonsky, *900 Shows a Year*, p. 116.

15. Palonsky, *900 Shows a Year*, p. 117.

16. Palmer, *The Courage to Teach*, p. 38.

17. Howard Zinn, *The Zinn Reader: Writings on Disobedience and Democracy* (New York: Seven Stories Press, 1997), p. 503.

18. Zinn, *The Zinn Reader*, p. 503.

19. Paulo Freire, *Pedagogy of Freedom: Ethics, Democracy, and Civic Courage* (Lanham, MD: Rowman and Littlefield, 1998), p. 101.

20. Gayathri Vaidyanathan, "Big Gap between What Scientists Say and Americans Think about Climate Change: But the Gap may be Closing between Scientists and the Public on Global Warming." *Scientific American*, January 30, 2015. Retrieved from https://www.scientificamerican.com/article/big-gap-between-what-scientists-say-and-americans-think-about-climate-change/, April 10, 2020.

21. Jennifer De Pinto, Fred Backus, Anthony Salvanto, "Most Americans Say Climate Change should be Addressed Now—CBS Poll." *CBS News*, September 15, 2019. Retrieved from https://www.cbsnews.com/news/cbs-news-poll-most-americans-say-climate-change-should-be-addressed-now-2019-09-15/, April 10, 2020.

22. Jamie Ballard, "45% of Americans Believe that Ghosts and Demons Exist." YouGov. Retrieved from https://today.yougov.com/topics/lifestyle/articles-reports/2019/10/21/paranormal-beliefs-ghosts-demons-poll, April 10, 2020.

23. Kurt Andersen, *Fantasyland: How America Went Haywire, A 500-Year History* (New York: Random House, 2017), p. 129.

24. Katie Mettler, "'Good Trouble': How John Lewis Fuses New and Old Tactics to Teach about Civil Disobedience." *The Washington Post*, June 23, 2016. Retrieved from https://www.washingtonpost.com/news/morning-mix/wp/2016/06/23/good-trouble-how-john-lewis-fuses-new-and-old-tactics-to-teach-about-civil-disobedience/, April 7, 2020.

25. Katherine Lymn and Alison Dirr, "Rep. John Lewis to Grads: Get into 'good trouble.'" *USA Today*, June 14, 2015. Retrieved from https://www.usatoday.com/story/news/nation/2015/06/14/rep-john-lewis-to-grads-get-into-good-trouble/71226886/, April 7, 2020.

26. Lymn and Dirr, "Rep. Lewis to Grads."

27. Medea Benjamin, "America Dropped 26,171 Bombs in 2016: What a Bloody End to Obama's Reign." *The Guardian*, January 9, 2017. Retrieved from https://www.theguardian.com/commentisfree/2017/jan/09/america-dropped-26171-bombs-2016-obama-legacy, April 9, 2020.

28. Hazrat Inayat Khan, *Sufi Teachings Book 1: The Way of Illumination* (Commodius Vicus e-Publisher, 2012), Location 916.

29. Khan, *The Way of Illumination*, location 927.

30. James W. Loewen, *Lies My Teacher Told Me: Everything Your American History Textbook Got Wrong* (New York: Touchstone, 1995), p. 12.

31. Jeff Z. Klein, "A Sidekick's Little-known Leading Role." *The New York Times*, September 1, 2013. Sunday, late edition, Section SP; Column 0; Sports Desk p.13.

32. Vine Deloria, Jr., *Custer Died for Your Sins: An Indian Manifesto* (Norman, OK: University of Oklahoma Press, 1969), p. 200.

33. Deloria, Jr., *Custer Died for Your Sins*, p. 200.

34. Deloria, Jr., *Custer Died for Your Sins*, pp. 200–201.

35. Deloria, Jr., *Custer Died for Your Sins*, p. 201.

36. Jeff Z. Klein, "A Sidekick's Little-known Leading Role."

37. Jeff Z. Klein, "A Sidekick's Little-known Leading Role."

38. "Jay Silverheels, Actor, 62, Dead; Was Tonto in TV 'Lone Ranger.'" *The New York Times*, March 6, 1980; ProQuest Historical Newspapers: *The New York Times*, p. D19.

39. Jeff Z. Klein, "A Sidekick's Little-known Leading Role."

40. DeNeen L. Brown, "In Search of an Uncomfortable Truth." *The Washington Post*, March 22, 2020.

41. Brown, "In Search of an Uncomfortable Truth."

42. Doha Madani, "Possible Mass Grave from 1921 Tulsa Race Massacre Found by Researchers." *NBC News*, December 16, 2019. Retrieved from https://www.nbcnews.com/news/nbcblk/possible-mass-grave-1921-tulsa-race-massacre-found-researchers-n1102781, April 14, 2020.

43. Brown, "In Search of an Uncomfortable Truth."
44. Brown, "In Search of an Uncomfortable Truth."
45. Brown, "In Search of an Uncomfortable Truth."
46. Vanessa Romo, "New Research Identifies Possible Mass Graves from 1921 Tulsa Race Massacre." National Public Radio, December 17, 2019. Retrieved from https://www.npr.org/2019/12/17/789015343/new-research-identifies-possible-mass-graves-from1921-tulsa-race-massacre, April 14, 2020.
47. Romo, "New Research Identifies Possible Mass Graves."
48. Brown, "In Search of an Uncomfortable Truth."
49. Brown, "In Search of an Uncomfortable Truth."
50. Ralph Waldo Emerson, *Selected Writings of Ralph Waldo Emerson* (New York: The Modern Library, 1992), p. 953.
51. Martin Luther King, Jr., *A Testament of Hope: The Essential Writings and Speeches of Martin Luther King, Jr.*, James M. Washington, Ed. (New York: HarperOne, 1986), p. 284.
52. King, *A Testament of Hope*, p. 284.
53. King, *A Testament of Hope*, p. 284.
54. King, *A Testament of Hope*, pp. 284–285.

CHAPTER 8

Issues and Trends

Sao Paulo's new director of education must have marveled at the surrealness of it all. It had been a long and difficult road. By 1988, Paulo Freire was one of the most influential educational thinkers of the twentieth century. He was world-renowned and respected, and more than qualified to hold the position. But to be leading an effort for education in Brazil was, for Freire, a remarkable turnabout twenty-five years in the making. In 1964, following the military coup that overthrew the democratically elected government of President Joao Goulart, Freire found himself imprisoned as a dissident for his radical and suddenly dangerous views on education.

Upon his eventual release, he was exiled from his home country for more than two decades. Prior to the coup, Freire had been one of the leading lights of Brazilian education. Then, virtually overnight, he became a criminal. The coup did not occur in a vacuum, of course. It was a presidential election year in the United States, and Lyndon Johnson feared Brazil becoming a second Cuba.

Goulart was seen as a threat by powerful multinational corporations that had friends in the Johnson administration and the Pentagon; it was the height of the Cold War. Combined with Brazil's own domestic politics, these produced a reaction that would derail Freire's important work with Brazil's children and youth. He would be exiled physically, and his words were banned.

Paulo Freire was not the first, nor the last, educator to have politics and world events enter his classroom. Politics and political agendas always encircle the educational endeavor; just ask Socrates. Too many teachers, however, are unprepared for the political nature of their job, and are therefore poorly equipped to confront these political forces. While most graduate schools of education require at least one course on this subject, often blandly called "Issues and Trends" in the course catalogue, undergraduate teacher preparation programs, it seems, rarely do.

Given the powerful forces arrayed against public schools, this is malpractice. Every teacher preparation program should spend time focusing on the societal role and purpose of schooling as well as arming teachers for the debates and the battles to come. Colleges of education must drive home the point that teaching is a political act with political and cultural ramifications.

We must do all we can to encourage future teachers to become voracious readers and wise consumers of information. We must insist on reminding future teachers that their job is not only to create active citizens but *they* must be active, informed, engaged citizens. A teacher who is not also an activist fails her students. W. E. B. DuBois correctly stated that "teachers, then, cannot be pedants or dilettantes; they cannot be mere technicians and higher artisans; they have got to be social statesmen and statesmen of high order."[1]

I believe all educators should view our vocations as Freire did. He called his work a "politico-pedagogical career."[2] Most of my students are at the end of their formal classwork—they are seniors in their last semester prior to student teaching. Each semester I write the word "Koch" on the board and ask if any of them have heard of or know about the Koch brothers? ALEC? Invariably, the answer is no.

They understand vaguely that there are shadowy figures and groups seeking to undermine public education, and that governments across the country have slashed support for schools, teachers, and public school families. All have an understanding that their pay will be disgraceful, that tenure is under assault, and that budgets get tighter each and every year. But they have no clue about the well-funded and coordinated web of malevolent actors and their political puppets. In spite of the outsize influence of these individuals and their organizations, my students have not been introduced to the Kochs, or the Devos family, or the Mercers.

They are unaware of the well-funded networks and their agendas. Some have a foggy notion of what words like *privatization*, *school choice*, and *standardization* mean, but only in slippery, academic terms. They are blissfully unaware how these phrases and their philosophies will impact every single day of their classroom career. In this chapter, I am going to look at two particular issues—the outsized power of the multinational conglomerate Pearson, and the undermining and re-segregation of public schools through charter schools—and their political contexts and consequences for educators.

Future teachers in colleges of education are caught up in these issues but are not given the chance to dig deep into them and to discover the political forces behind them. In this, colleges of education fail our students. Before we look at these issues, though, we must investigate the ideology that powers them both. I write this word, too, on my board.

This ideology is one of the market forces and business models. It is an ideology that reduces man's intellect to a set of marketable skills. It is an ideology that fundamentally views education as a private commodity rather than a public good. It is an ideology that seeks as its ultimate outcome the complete privatization of the American school system. It is an ideology that for more than three decades now has denigrated teachers, undermined school systems, and sought—piece by piece—to dismantle public education. This ideology has a name "neoliberalism."

Neoliberalism is described by Ben Tarnoff as "the idea that everything should be run as a business—that market metaphors, metrics, and practices should permeate all fields of human life."[3] In this worldview teachers are technicians, grades are data or metrics, students are commodities, and schools are factories. Freire describes the "scourge of neoliberalism, with its cynical fatalism and its inflexible negation of the right to dream differently, to dream of utopia."[4]

Robert W. McChesney points out, "It is precisely in its oppression of nonmarket forces that we see how neoliberalism operates not only as an economic system, but as a political and cultural system as well."[5] A *Bloomberg* article on Pearson by Leonid Bershidsky mentions "the education business" three times, an "education conglomerate" once, and the "e-learning industry" once.[6] The language of education has been conquered by neoliberal jargon. And those who control the language control the debate.

In the neoliberal educational order, schools produce workers, not citizens. The implications of surrendering to this warped ideal are staggering to comprehend and yet too many undergraduate teacher education students are not asked or allowed to wrestle with these implications. Neoliberalism views America's schools as a minor league for corporate America.

The view is perfectly captured by former Exxon-Mobile CEO and US Secretary of State Rex Tillerson. Tillerson, a bear of a man with a drawl as thick as Texas toast, once said,

> "I'm not sure public schools understand that we're their customer—that we, the business community, are your customer. What they don't understand is they are producing a product at the end of that high school graduation. . . . Now is that product in a form that we, the customer, can use it? Or is it defective, and we're not interested?"[7]

Students who do not meet the needs of corporate America are, in this equation, "defective."

Tillerson continued saying American schools "have got to step up the performance level—or they're basically turning out defective products that have no future."[8] They are not useful to big businesses. Dewey feared this educational ideal a century ago, darkly prophesying an education model where the student "is trained like an animal rather than educated like a human being."[9] Perhaps in the safe and staid atmosphere of a graduate school seminar, this sentence is a platitude; but in the context of neoliberalism and the battle to dismantle our public school system, these words are chilling.

Under this ideology of business models, one business in particular has benefited. Under Presidents George W. Bush and Barack Obama, Pearson Education became a behemoth and served as something of a shadow Department of Education. Along with McGraw-Hill and Houghton Mifflin Harcourt, Pearson is one of the so-called "Big Three" publishing houses that control more than 85 percent of the educational material market in the United States.[10] A report in *Wired* ominously noted that "Pearson would like to become education's first major conglomerate" and compared the company to "Big Pharma."[11]

New York Times columnist Gail Collins noted in 2012 that

> an American child could go to a public school run by Pearson, studying from books produced by Pearson, while his or her progress is evaluated by Pearson standardized tests. The only public participant in the show would be the taxpayer.[12]

Collins goes on to ask, "when No Child Left Behind was passed...do you recall anybody mentioning that it would provide monster profits for the private business sector?"[13] In February 2001, Peter Jovanovich, then CEO of Pearson Education, could barely contain his joy, like the proverbial cat that had caught the canary.

Jovanovich boasted that George W. Bush's signature educational policy, No Child Left Behind (NCLB), "almost reads like our business plan."[14] Indeed, in the decade after passage of NCLB Pearson Education's profits increased 175 percent.[15] *Politico* investigated Pearson's web of contracts and services and concluded that the corporation "writes the textbooks and tests that drive instruction in public schools across the nation."[16] Its North American division does an astonishing $4 billion in sales annually, which, as *Politico* noted, accounts for half of the company's total profits.[17]

American students are a captive and exceptionally lucrative "market." Pearson utilizes these profits to employ "aggressive lobbyists, top-notch marketing and a highly skilled sales team."[18] Pearson even established a charitable foundation that "made a practice of treating school officials from across the nation to trips abroad, to conferences where the only education company represented was Pearson."[19] This continued until 2013, when the attorney general of the state of New York forced an end to the practice.

My teacher preparation students know Pearson intimately because, in addition to having expanded unchecked into nearly all levels of K-12 education across the nation, Pearson also has gained an insidious foothold in higher education. They have managed this through EdTPA, a new "assessment" system for pre-service teachers that will make Pearson Education the gatekeeper of who will teach the children of North Carolina and many other states. Not content to control the curriculum and assessment of K-12 education, Pearson now intends to control the teachers themselves by controlling the curriculum and the "final exam" of teacher preparation program.

Colleges of Education will be conveyors of Pearson's ideas and criterion; de facto employees of Pearson Education. A private, very much for-profit multinational corporation is in charge of the preparation of many state's future teachers. Pearson, not the faculty of our programs, will decide who becomes a teacher and who does not. My students are well aware that EdTPA is a betrayal of the college's mission and proclaimed ideals.

They know it is a waste of their time and their money. They know it has no actual bearing on what kind of teacher they will become. What they often do not know, however, is the dangerous agenda that undergirds EdTPA. That's where we have failed them. Denied the opportunity to study or question this "assessment" and the ideology that sustains it, future teachers are intellectually gagged and compelled into a stifling silence.

Such silence is compounded when future teachers are driven by their program to become active participants in the dismantling of public schools. Future teachers at several North Carolina colleges of education have been drafted into the effort to re-segregate our schools under the guise of school reform and "choice" through HB 1030—the University of North Carolina Laboratory Schools measure—passed in 2016.

Initial messages out of Raleigh about partnering with struggling schools and developing "lab schools" were deeply misleading; when the actual legislation was put into practice, North Carolina colleges of education were called upon to dismantle neighborhood schools and replace them with charter schools.

Students and families currently attending these schools were not guaranteed they could return to these transformed community schools even if they wanted to, being forced instead to apply to become enrolled in their new school and, while many were told they would receive "priority," in placements, no one knew what that meant in practice.

One of these schools was Middle Fork Elementary School in Winston Salem, which was taken over by my institution, Appalachian State University (ASU), before the 2018–2019 school year. Though Middle Fork served 358 students at the time ASU took over, we accepted only 300 students for our new "academy."[20] The other 58 children and their families had to find a new school.

Since coming under Republican control in 2011, the legislature of the state of North Carolina has abused and attacked public education, public schools, and public school teachers. It is disheartening to say the least to see the state's colleges of education cowardly cooperating with and advancing these attacks on public school teachers. When ASU took over the operation of Middle Fork it summarily *dismissed the entire school faculty*, lending its imprimatur to the disgraceful fiction that the teachers had failed their students.

The teachers were invited to reapply, though without any guarantee of employment. This was a degrading and belittling way to treat professional educators, as evidenced by the fact that "of the 45 staff members at Middle Fork Academy, only 18 returned" following the ASU takeover.[21] *The Winston Salem Journal* quoted a Middle Fork parent complaining that teachers at the school were "not working hard enough."[22]

The *Journal* also dutifully spouted all the negative data it could find to fill out the picture of a school with an incompetent and failing faculty—"a Title I school which received an F school-performance grade for the 2016–2017 school year," "third graders scored about 27 percent proficiency on end-of-grade tests on reading," and so on.[23]

Among all the statistics, however, the *Journal* did not mention socioeconomic data that might also be important. Like the state legislature, the *Journal* placed blame solely on the teachers, students, and families of Middle Fork. However, professional educators understand that it matters that an astonishing 99.1 percent of students at Middle Fork qualified for free or reduced lunch.[24] This level of poverty is the result of our Dickensian state government officials and their war on the poor and people of color in our state, not the dedicated men and women of Middle Fork Elementary School.

Rather than replace these dedicated educators at Middle Fork, perhaps ASU might have considered using our scholarship and our stewardship to advocate against the ignorant and destructive policies that have made North Carolina tenth in the nation in overall poverty, tenth in the nation in highest child poverty rates, tied for twelfth in the nation for highest "deep poverty" rate, and worst in the nation in 2014–2015 in per-pupil expenditure (dropping $250/student).[25]

The legislature also made the Old North State, "46th in teacher pay . . . [and] North Carolina teachers earn nearly $10,000 less than the national average."[26] State funds for books were cut 80 percent, 5,200 teacher and 3,850 teacher assistant positions were eliminated while student population grew.[27] These are the reasons schools fail—not the children, not the parents, and not the teachers.

ASU insulted professional educators while taking no issue with the underlying factors affecting the students and families at Middle Fork: namely a state where three times more African American children than white lived in poverty, and where, according to the state's "A-F grading system [for schools], almost all high-poverty schools receive exceedingly poor grades [recall Middle Fork being saddled with an 'F' as a school], while almost all high-wealth schools excel."[28] No wonder *Education Week* called North Carolina's leaders as "The Most Backward Legislature in America" and lamented the state's "race to the bottom."[29]

There were also deep concerns about the racial implications of ASU taking over this particular school. Middle Fork's racial demographics at the time of the takeover were 50 percent African American, 32 percent Hispanic, 11 percent Caucasian, 3 percent Asian, and under 1percent American Indian.[30] ASU, meanwhile, was 84percent Caucasian, 3 percent African American, and 4 percent Hispanic when it took control of Middle Fork.[31] It would be virtually impossible to find a cooperating institution that looked less like its sister institution.

Just as troubling, faculty was a paltry 7 percent people of color.[32] Only 59 percent of ASU seniors reported having "often had serious conversations with students of a different race or ethnicity."[33] On July 4, 2017, the National Education Association said the following about charter schools:

> Charters have grown the most in school districts that were already struggling to meet students' needs due to longstanding, systemic and ingrained patterns of institutional neglect, racial and ethnic segregation, inequitable school funding, and disparities in staff, programs and services.
>
> The result has been the creation of separate, largely unaccountable, privately managed charter school systems in those districts that undermine support and funding of local public schools. Such separate and unequal education

systems are disproportionately located in, and harm, students and communities of color by depriving both of the high quality public education system that should be their right.[34]

Though participating institutions and many educators have insistently cooperated with the Orwellian labeling of these new schools as "laboratory schools," Representative Craig Horn, cochair of the North Carolina House's K-12 Committee, said the quiet part out loud, admitting, "For all practical purposes, a lab school is a charter school."[35] Thus, colleges of education have allowed themselves to become the engines of privatization and are instruments of a neo-Jim Crow system that goes against every professed mission and ideal of these colleges.

This is not hyperbole. In 2017, the *Raleigh News and Observer* published a study that found "charter schools in North Carolina are more segregated than traditional public schools and have more affluent students."[36] A 2019 report by the North Carolina Justice Center (NCJC) that examined a decade of data found that the "number of racially and economically isolated schools has increased" and that "Charter schools tend to exacerbate segregation."[37]

The report starkly states, "The growing share of racially and economically isolated schools should be a warning sign that our school system is becoming more unequal, not less."[38] In the years examined by the NCJC, "The share of students of color [increased] from 44 percent of all traditional public school students to over 51 percent."[39] And yet, as the state became more diverse, the school system reverted to a pre-Brown stance.

These racial concerns were born out by the very selection of Appalachian State to take over a school in Winston Salem. While ASU looked nothing like Middle Fork, Winston Salem State (WSU) did. WSU is 72 percent African American and 16 percent Caucasian.[40] WSS also has a terrific teacher preparation program, and is *five-and-a-half miles away* from Middle Fork. ASU is, by comparison, *92 miles away*. WSS was not asked to work with the children five miles away, of course, because the North Carolina state legislature has spent years attacking and undermining the state's historically black colleges and universities (HBCUs).

It takes a special kind of willful blindness not to see that ASU is being used as a cudgel to undermine WSS. It is especially problematic that a college of education so busy braying its commitment to diversity and inclusion is increasing segregated education in Forsyth County, which is "among the 10 most segregated districts [in North Carolina], as measured by racial dissimilarity."[41]

The county is also "among the 10-most economically segregated districts in the state."[42] Perhaps the most damning piece of data is that, in 72 percent of North Carolina counties that have at least one charter school, "charter schools increase the degree of racial segregation in the district, as measured by the racial dissimilarity index."⁴³ This is not education, and we are called upon to name it for what it is called "colonialism."

ASU Chancellor Sheri Everts proclaimed, "The Academy will be a living laboratory of educational research, collaboration, outreach and impact that will be life-changing for more than 300 K-8 students who will be reminded daily that a college education can become their reality."⁴⁴ The legislation does, indeed, call for finding best practices through the work at the schools; but having replaced students and faculty, increased funding ("They [the lab/charter schools] also get support from UNC, with a $2 million annual budget specially allocated by the legislature.") been given "flexibility and independent decision-making," what possible lessons could be drawn?⁴⁵

Give up on a school and have it taken over by outsiders? If the desire had actually been to discover best practices for improving student experience and performance at Middle Fork, ASU would have to work with the students, families, faculty, and staff that were there—not create a new school from scratch and attempt to make invalid comparisons.

As for Everts's promise of "outreach" and "collaboration," the legislation calls for an advisory board, but the makeup shows the contempt for the community—all members are selected by the chancellor (who lives more than an hour away), and the board is to be comprised of the chancellor, the college dean, a member of the board of trustees, two college faculty, the local school superintendent, and, almost as an afterthought, "A member of the community who resides in the local school administrative unit in which the laboratory school is located."⁴⁶

A *member of the community.* Continuing the top-down, white savior aspect of the legislation, even the course of study for the school is to be decided upon by the chancellor. The superintendent of Columbus County schools in Eastern North Carolina recalled of his community's lab/charter school, "We were asked to give up our entire school with no involvement in it. It's like we really were not needed."⁴⁷ There is hardly more collaboration with the school's new faculty, only half of whom, according to the legislation, need even be licensed.

The curriculum at Middle Fork after the takeover is designed by an ASU alumnus and then handed down to the teachers. "Teachers . . . are free to give input," one generally favorable article noted.⁴⁸ A first-grade teacher said,

> "They come in and they say, 'We want you to try this and here's why. . . . Tell us what you need to do this. How can we help you?' That's amazing. You don't get that in a lot of other places. . . . They treat us like professionals."⁴⁹

It is a testament to the state of teaching in North Carolina that a teacher could be reduced to the role of acting out someone else's lesson plan and consider this being treated like a professional.

∽

In the early summer of 1974, the Nixon administration was unraveling. For the president's dear friend and confidant, the evangelical revivalist Billy Graham, this was a personal disappointment and also a professional quandary. Graham had all but given Nixon a full-throated endorsement in 1972 and had defended the embattled incumbent throughout the Watergate controversy.

Now, however, Nixon's tapes were out (redacted versions, at least), and there was little room for the defense of a man who came across as paranoid, embittered, corrupt, vile, and utterly dishonest. The tapes revealed a man enmeshed with a cast of characters as unethical and immoral as they were comically inept. Moreover, the tapes revealed a Nixon who committed crimes against the constitution and moved to cover up these crimes with no compunction. Nixon had thrown the nation into its gravest constitutional crisis since the Civil War. Billy Graham, though, was most bothered by Nixon's potty mouth.

"I just didn't know that he used that kind of language," Graham told reporters, clutching his pearls.[50]

To be fair to Graham, even television news executives, according to the *New York Times*, were troubled by Nixon's language, worrying that, for their nightly news broadcasts, the president's "profanity may pose a problem."[51] Still, with so much evidence of so many crimes, Graham's focus on the president's dirty words stands out. His myopic vision reminds us of the old saying about not seeing the forest for the trees, and it is also too reminiscent of the way many educators view the politics of our work.

It is far too easy for a teacher to become so caught up with and overwhelmed by the day-to-day struggle with testing, planning, standards, discipline, administrators, parents, and so much else, that we lose sight of the bigger picture. Like Reverend Graham, we focus on the small to the detriment of larger forces and issues. There is a concerted, supremely well-funded effort to destroy America's public schools and our commitment to public education. Future teachers must be made aware of the many groups, think tanks, and wealthy individuals who are seeking to undermine their vocation and their ability to do their job.

Teachers must commit to being informed and active. Staying up-to-date on pedagogy while ignoring politics is a terrible mistake. To discuss the standardization of the American mind without talking about the role American business interests play in our schools is foolish. To even pretend to discuss American schools since the Reagan years without understanding neoliberalism is to be a fraud. One organization alone, the Koch-aligned Council (ALEC), puts elected leaders and business titans into the same room where, incredibly, lawmakers are provided with ready-made, right-wing legislation.

The officials then dutifully return home, introduce, and pass the bills. Jane Mayer notes that critics call ALEC a "bill mill," and that the organization "produced about a thousand new bills a year, some two hundred of which became state law."[52] One of those state laws that began in the bowels of ALEC was HB 1030. Teachers—new and veteran alike—must be informed about these dark groups seeking to control our classrooms. Teachers know we are in a fight for our schools; we cannot possibly win if we do not fully know our opponents.

The powers working against our school systems force educators to decide whether America's public schools will continue to be incubators of democracy or will become engines for oligarchy. Let the line we draw be bright as the morning sun—when the dust settles (if, indeed there is any dust kicked up), we will all be held to account and we will all have to take a stand. Moral declarations are deeply uncomfortable places for scholars. We are trained to be open, thoughtful, and objective. However, now is the time to speak and to act, as both educators and citizens.

This is not a pedagogical crisis, or a methodological or technical or professional or even a purely political crisis. *This is a moral crisis*. It must be no surprise to those who have advocated a strong and vibrant public school system as a bulwark of democratic ideals and traditions that, as our public schools have been steadily undermined, so has our nation. Martin Gilens of Princeton University and Benjamin I. Page of Northwestern University published a study in 2014 asserting that the United States had ceased to be a functioning democracy and was now an oligarchy.

Nicholas Kristoff of the *New York Times* summarized their findings by noting that Gilens and Page "examined 1,779 policy issues and found that attitudes of wealthy people and of business groups mattered a great deal to the final outcome — but that preferences of average citizens were almost irrelevant."[53] In the words of the study, "In the United States . . . the majority does not rule."[54] America's democratic crisis should not be divorced from turning our back on our commitment to a vibrant, *public* school system.

Being educators who are aware of and involved with politics will often lead to controversy. So be it. Once we walk into our classroom, we walk into this fight. The best mantra, unsurprisingly, comes to us from Freire who, home from exile, wrote:

> I am a teacher who stands up for what is right against what is indecent, who is in favor of freedom against authoritarianism, who is a supporter of authority against freedom with no limits, and who is a defender of democracy against the dictatorship of the right or left. I am a teacher who favors the permanent struggle against every form of bigotry and against the economic domination of individuals and social classes. I am a teacher who rejects the present system of capitalism, responsible for the aberration of misery in the midst of plenty. I am a teacher full of hope, in spite of all signs to the contrary.[55]

You are not a politician but, like Freire, you *are* a teacher, and politics comes with the job.

Notes

1. W.E.B. DuBois, *The Education of Black People: Ten Critiques, 1906-1960*, Herbert Aptheker, Ed. (New York: Monthly Review Press, 1973), p. 78.
2. Paulo Freire, *Pedagogy of Freedom: Ethics, Democracy, and Civic Courage* (Lanham, MD: Rowman and Littlefield, 1998), p. 37.
3. Ben Tarnoff, "Neoliberalism Turned Our World into a Business: And there Are Two Big Winners." *The Guardian*, December 13, 2016. Retrieved from https://www.theguardian.com/us-news/2016/dec/13/donald-trump-silicon-valley-leaders-neoliberalism-administration, April 17, 2020.
4. Freire, *Pedagogy of Freedom*, p. 22.
5. Robert W. McChesney, "Introduction." In Noam Chomsky's *Profit Over People: Neoliberalism and Global Order* (New York: Seven Stories Press, 1999), Location 57 Kindle edition.
6. Leonid Bershidsky, "Why the Financial Times Has a New Owner." *Bloomberg*, July 24, 2015. Retrieved from https://www.bloomberg.com/opinion/articles/2015-07-24/why-the-financial-times-has-a-new-owner, April 17, 2020.
7. Valerie Strauss, "Why Education Activists Are Furious at ExxonMobil's CEO." *The Washington Post*, December 29, 2015. Retrieved from https://www.washingtonpost.com/news/answer-sheet/wp/2015/12/27/why-education-activists-are-furious-at-exxonmobils-ceo/, April 29, 2020.
8. Strauss, "Why Education Activists Are Furious."
9. John Dewey, *Democracy and Education* (New York: The Free Press, 1916), p. 13.
10. Davis, "No Test Left Behind." *TPM Features*. N.D. Retrieved from https://talkingpointsmemo.com/features/privatization/four/, April 19, 2020.
11. Anya Kamenetz, "Pearson's Quest to Cover the Planet in Company-Run Schools." *Wired*, April 12, 2016. Retrieved from https://www.wired.com/2016/04/apec-schools/, April 17, 2020.

12. Gail Collins, "A Very Pricey Pineapple." *New York Times*, April 27, 2012. Retrieved from https://www.nytimes.com/2012/04/28/opinion/collins-a-very-pricey-pineapple.html, April 17, 2020.

13. Collins, "A Very Pricey Pineapple."

14. Davis, "No Test Left Behind."

15. Davis, "No Test Left Behind."

16. Stephanie Simon, "No Profit Left Behind: In the High-Stakes World of American Education, Pearson makes Money Even when Its Results don't Measure Up." *Politico*, February 10, 2015. Retrieved from https://www.politico.com/story/2015/02/pearson-education-115026_Page2.html, April 17, 2020.

17. Simon, "No Profit Left Behind."

18. Simon, "No Profit Left Behind."

19. Simon, "No Profit Left Behind."

20. Sarah Newell, "Middle Fork to Partner with App State for School Conversion in 2018-2019." *The Winston Salem Journal*, November 7, 2017. Retrieved from https://www.journalnow.com/news/local/middle-fork-to-partner-with-app-state-for-school-conversion-in-2018-19/article_e8971ced-3412-53f0-bfa8-8ff5d8b322c5.html, May 2, 2020.

21. Lindsay Marchello and Kari Travis, "UNC Lab Schools Changing Formula for Education." *The Enquirer-Journal* (Monroe, NC). Section News, June 11, 2019.

22. Newell, "Middle Fork to Partner with App State for School Conversion in 2018-2019."

23. Newell, "Middle Fork to Partner with App State for School Conversion in 2018-2019."

24. "Middle Fork Elementary School Profile." Retrieved from https://www.schooldigger.com/go/NC/schools/0150002728/school.aspx, July 3, 2020.

25. Deborah R. Gerhardt, "Pay Our Teachers or Lose Your Job: North Carolina is Pushing Its Best Educators Out. We have to do Something." *Slate*, January 5, 2014. Retrieved from https://slate.com/human-interest/2014/01/north-carolinas-assault-on-teachers-has-to-stop.html, May 2, 2020.

26. Gerhardt, "Pay Our Teachers or Lose Your Job."

27. Gerhardt, "Pay Our Teachers or Lose Your Job."

28. Gene Nichol, *Indecent Assembly: The North Carolina Legislature's Blueprint for the War on Democracy and Equality* (Durham, NC: Blair, 2020), pp. 14–15.

29. John Wilson, "The Most Backward Legislature in America." *Education Week*, July 29, 2013. Retrieved from http://blogs.edweek.org/edweek/john_wilson_unleashed/2013/07/the_most_backward_legislature_in_america.html, May 2, 2020.

30. "Middle Fork Elementary School Profile." Retrieved from https://www.schooldigger.com/go/NC/schools/0150002728/school.aspx, July 3, 2020.

31. "Appalachian State University College Portrait: Undergraduate Snapshot." Retrieved from http://www.collegeportraits.org/NC/Appalachian/print, May 2, 2020.

32. "Appalachian State University College Portrait: Appalachian Classes and Instructors." Retrieved from http://www.collegeportraits.org/NC/Appalachian/print, May 2, 2020.

33. "Appalachian State University College Portrait: Experiences with Diverse Groups of People and Ideas." Retrieved from http://www.collegeportraits.org/NC/Appalachian/print, May 2, 2020.

34. 2017 National Education Association Representative Assembly, "NEA Policy Statement on Charter Schools." July 2017. Retrieved from https://ra.nea.org/nea-policy-statement-charter-schools/, May 2, 2020.

35. Billy Ball, "Despite Backing of Legislature and UNC Leaders, Critics Worry NC's Lab School Experiment is Doomed to Failure." *NC Policy Watch*, February 7, 2018. Retrieved from http://www.ncpolicywatch.com/2018/02/07/despite-backing-legislature-unc-leaders-critics-worry-ncs-lab-school-experiment-doomed-failure/, July 9, 2020.

36. Nichol, *Indecent Assembly*, p. 22.

37. Kris Nordstrom, *Stymied by Segregation: How Integration Can Transform North Carolina Schools and the Lives of Its Students* (Raleigh, NC: North Carolina Justice Center, 2019), p. 1.

38. Nordstrom, *Stymied by Segregation*, p. 5.

39. Nordstrom, *Stymied by Segregation*, p. 6.

40. "Winston Salem State University College Portrait: Undergraduate Snapshot." Retrieved from http://www.collegeportraits.org/NC/WSSU/print, May 2, 2020.

41. Nordstrom, *Stymied by Segregation*, p. 8.

42. Nordstrom, *Stymied by Segregation*, p. 8.

43. Nordstrom, *Stymied by Segregation*, p. 12.

44. Ball, "Despite Backing of Legislature and UNC Leaders."

45. Marchello and Travis, "UNC Lab Schools Changing Formula for Education."

46. "Article 29A: University of North Carolina Laboratory Schools." Retrieved from https://www.ncleg.gov/EnactedLegislation/Statutes/PDF/ByArticle/Chapter_116/Article_29A.pdf, July 9, 2020.

47. Ball, "Despite Backing of Legislature and UNC Leaders."

48. Marchello and Travis, "UNC Lab Schools Changing Formula for Education."

49. Marchello and Travis, "UNC Lab Schools Changing Formula for Education."

50. Francis Fitzgerald, *The Evangelicals: The Struggle to Shape America* (New York: Simon and Schuster, 2017), p. 256.

51. Les Brown, "TV Weighs using Nixon Tapes; Profanity May Pose a Problem." *New York Times* (1923-Current file); New York, NY [New York, NY] May 15, 1974: 90. Retrieved on July 11, 2020.

52. Jane Mayer, *Dark Money: The Hidden History of the Billionaires Behind the Rise of the Radical Right* (New York: Anchor Books, 2017), pp. 425–426.

53. Nicholas Kristof, "Government vs. The People." *Herald-Tribune*, January 21, 2016. Retrieved from https://www.heraldtribune.com/article/LK/20160121/Opinion/605202155/SH/, April 28, 2020.

54. Kristof, "Government vs. The People."

55. Freire, *Pedagogy of Freedom*, p. 63.

CHAPTER 9

A Vocation at Risk

Outflanking the Forty-eight

In May 1865, the Civil War was all but over. April had seen both the final surrender of Robert E. Lee's Army of Northern Virginia and the murder of Abraham Lincoln. The Radical Republicans in Congress, led by the indomitable Thaddeus Stevens, made preparations to wrest control of the postwar nation from the new president, Andrew Johnson. In New York, veteran abolitionists gathered for the thirty-second annual meeting of the American Anti-Slavery Society. The major item on the agenda was a simple one: whether or not to disband the organization.

The legendary abolitionist William Lloyd Garrison was the leader of the disband faction, arguing that it was "an absurdity to maintain an antislavery society after slavery is dead."[1] Frederick Douglass believed such naivete was dangerous, particularly for his people still in the South, arguing that it would be far more prudent to "wait and see what new form this old monster will assume."[2] The final vote was 118-48 to continue the organization with a focus on the political, civil, and human rights of the recently freed former slaves.

Those forty-eight abolitionists who believed the fight was over are the ultimate cautionary tale for America's teachers. Bless their little hearts, those dewy-eyed forty-eight abolitionists who thought that military victory would usher in something like instant equality were criminally misinformed. Freedom on paper is hardly the same as freedom in practice. Douglass and others understood that the war was entering a new phase, and that winning the freedom was equally important to having won the war. The forty-eight took far too much for granted, and in this they are our lesson.

To protect this sacred vocation of ours, teachers must admit that there are many things we can no longer take for granted. Not everyone supports public education, not everyone believes in the work we do, and there are dedicated forces working against us. Indeed, my use of the words "this sacred vocation of ours" would have no doubt engendered an angry dissent from R. J. Rushdoony, who scoldingly titled his seminal work *The Messianic Character of American Education* and greatly disapproved of the notion that the American system of education should prepare students to be critical thinkers in a participatory democracy.

Rushdoony, known in some circle as "America's foremost critic of public education," believed that American schools should assist in creating a theocratic, Christian society, not a pluralistic one.[3] Rushdoony feared democracy, writing, "Democracy always perishes from an overdose of democracy."[4]

While many educators deceive ourselves into taking for granted Dewey's role as a sort-of secular saint of the United States, Rushdoony despised the man, writing,

> his theory, based on an implicit and unreasoning dogmatism, unleashed a new Islam into American education and philosophy, savagely intolerant, belligerently contemptuous of all previous learning and thought, and dedicated to an educational jargon unfamiliar and irrational to all who were not devotees of this new Mohammed.[5]

Where Dewey could write, "a thought is not a thought unless it is one's own," Rushdoony sought a system that imposed ecclesiastical "truths" on America's children, no matter their faith or lack thereof.[6]

Though Dewey is far more famous in teacher preparation programs, we must not take for granted the influence of Rushdoony's dash for madrassas in the United States. One of his acolytes Betsy DeVos became US Secretary of Education in 2017. DeVos and her husband have long contributed to organizations dedicated to blurring the line between church and state, and both agree with Rushdoony that, as Dick DeVos has said, "As we look at many communities in our country, the church has been displaced by the public school as the center for activity . . . [and] it is certainly our hope that more and more churches will get more and more active and engaged in education."[7]

When asked if private, Christian schools should continue to rely on private funding or receive taxpayer money, Betsy DeVos unapologetically replied, "There are not enough philanthropic dollars in America to fund what is currently the need in education. . . . Our desire is to confront the culture in ways that will continue to advance God's kingdom."[8]

Ms. DeVos has also been refreshingly forthright about her expectation when it comes to her family's "philanthropic" donations too: "My family is the biggest contributor of soft money to the Republican National Committee," she has written. "I have decided to stop taking offense at the suggestion that we are trying to buy influence. Now I simply concede the point. They are right. We do expect something in return. . . . We expect a return on our investment."[9] Teachers must not write such extremism off as mere cranks, and as DeVos's ascension to the leader of America's schools shows, we must no longer take for granted a belief in secular, pluralistic schools.

In a nation with more than 13 million children living in poverty, we cannot take for granted that our society wants what is best for our students.[10] Politicians who pronounce as heroes are worthless unless their vacuous praise comes with tangible policies, and so we must no longer take for granted that a leader or a political party will support education. We must demand that they *show* us their commitment.

We cannot assume that our administration supports our work: administrators unable or unwilling to advocate for their teachers, students, and community should be unceremoniously dumped. This wonderful, extraordinary job needs us all to recognize and be ready for the fights ahead. Our democracy needs strong public schools, and our public schools need teachers who understand the stakes. This vocation *is* at risk, and it deserves defenders and defending. The battle, though only just beginning, is not new. We are not the first generation of educators to confront superstition and hatred.

Edmonia Highgate was an African American school teacher and among the first educators for the newly freed slaves in the American South. In December 1866, she wrote from her new school in Louisiana's Lafayette Parish,

> There has been much opposition to the school. . . . Twice I have been shot at in my room. My night scholars have been shot, but none killed. The rebels here threatened to burn down the school and house in which I board.[11]

In Alabama, Savilla Edge conducted a school for the freed people in her home "until opponents of black education burned her house down."[12] Education in America has always been a profound battleground where reactionary forces fight against enlightenment and progress. In all likelihood, it will always be.

∞

The house had no air conditioning, and it was stifling, causing rivulets of sweat to trickle down faces, backs, and legs. The couple—married for more than four decades at the time—busied themselves cleaning and straightening. Saturdays were the one day they were both home from the cotton mill and it was dedicated to laundry, vacuuming, and bringing order to their dusty kingdom. They didn't own their own home and never would, so part of the cleaning was to keep the landlord happy and off their backs. She paused and leaned against the broom, wiping her face with the back of her hand.

"It's hotter than a June barn dance," he said.

"It's miserable hot," she agreed.

He looked her oversuspiciously for a moment, taking note of her attire for the first time that day.

"Well," he suggested, "take off them dungarees and put on some shorts."

She blushed and shook her head no with emphasis.

"I'd rather sweat," she said, looking away from his gaze.

"What?! Why?" he demanded. She stared at the floor. She didn't really want to admit the truth to him: she was deeply embarrassed for him to see her legs now that they were lined and crisscrossed with varicose veins. She had spent her adult life as a "puller" in the mills while he was a "fixer." She had spent most of her life on her feet, and her legs showed the results. With an uncharacteristically timid voice, she told him. He took her by the hand, pulled her onto his lap, and told her, "Garnell, all I ever see is the 16 year old girl I fell in love with."

That story was one of my grandma Bryant's favorite about my grandpa, because it reminded her of his gentle kindness. That afternoon was a little over two months before Grandpa received the diagnosis of cancer that would end his life a scant six weeks later. Their life together saw them raise four children, bury one of them, and struggle economically every day they were together. There was much love and laughter, but also a through-line of economic troubles and worries.

They were cotton mill workers; I am a college professor. Please do not misunderstand this statement; I am not as intelligent, decent, or wise as my grandparents. I am, though, more *educated*, and that difference has made my life easier, and has provided me with opportunities they never had. My family has made this economic progress thanks, primarily, to an American institution: public schools. That is why I am so passionate about and deeply committed to the ideal of democratic and equal public schools for every American child. For my family, public schools changed our world and our destiny.

Miss Inez Davenport also knew the power of schools and a good teacher. She knew and appreciated the political power and essence of education. Perhaps, that's why her student Barbara Johns felt comfortable coming to

Miss Davenport with her plans for a school strike. Though such a disruptive plan might be kept from most teachers, Miss Davenport was not your average teacher, nor was Barbara Johns an average student. The niece of civil rights activist Reverend Vernon Johns, Barbara's nascent activism should have been no surprise.

Still, though Barbara could have asked advice from the man who "later mentored Martin Luther King, Jr.," she instead, "never consulted her Montgomery uncle about the strike she was planning. Instead, the studious girl with the sparkling eyes and a luminous smile looked to her favorite teacher."[13] Freire demands that teachers be "coherent," which he defines as always working to narrow the gap between what we say and what we do; Barbara Johns demanded the same from her teacher, Miss Davenport.[14]

In class at Robert R. Morton High School in Farmville, Virginia, Johns and a group of frustrated students were complaining about their school facilities, which were so poor, "passersby imagined [them] to be chicken coops."[15] Morton was "built in 1939, [and] was badly overcrowded . . . it had no gymnasium or cafeteria. There were no locker rooms or showers—or late afternoon buses for those who wanted to play sports or engage in after-school activities."[16]

The students' concern that their school could be confused for a coop was hardly a paranoid delusion:

> To cope with the crowding, white authorities had attached a few wooden, tarpaper shacks to the main building. These leaked in the rain, and were heated by wood stoves that a black teacher, doubling as a bus driver, set and lighted in the winter months.[17]

As Miss Davenport listened to her students' frustrations, she "shared with them a news article about some Massachusetts students who had gone on strike and won over an issue that concerned them."[18]

The story sparked something in Barbara Johns—a feeling of determined hope. She stayed after class, further questioning Miss Davenport and, most importantly of all, seeking to discover "whether her teacher really meant what she had said."[19] Fearing reprisals from the white population, the local NAACP was hesitant to back the fight for educational equality and an end to the brutal, dehumanizing practice of segregation. Johns pushed ahead though, encouraged and supported by her teacher. The effort would be rolled into what is now known simply as the Brown v. Board of Education case that spurred a revolution in American society, and ushered in the second Reconstruction.

Are you absolutely certain that you want to become a teacher? That's the big question in the end: do you really want to take on this responsibility, and are you really up to the task? You surely understand that, barring some road-to-Damascus epiphany for those who make policy and set priorities, you will never be paid what you are worth. I assume that you know that there are those who believe that you are a teacher because you were not bright enough to do anything else.

They will look at you with a mix of pity and condescension when they learn what you do—and you have to put up with that for the remainder of your professional life. Can you handle all of that? Are you deeply idealistic and committed without question to the future of your nation? Do you fully understand the role of a teacher in a democratic society? Do you believe in the unlimited potential of young people to shape a more just and compassionate society? Are you up for constant challenges, and it is within you to rise to meet them on a consistent basis?

If you are not sure of the answer to these questions, then I beg you to travel across campus to the registrar's office and select for yourself a new major. If you are already in the classroom and cannot answer these questions in the affirmative, then I hope you will leave the classroom as soon as possible. Because the kind of commitment I have mentioned above is exactly what it takes to be a great teacher, and anything less is not to be tolerated for a job so deeply noble.

The title of this chapter is, of course, a tongue-in-cheek reference to the 1980s blue ribbon education panel report entitled *A Nation at Risk*. The report is as frightening as anything ever conceived in the mind of Poe or King, telling America that our educational system was deeply flawed and in need of serious reform. While there is certainly some truth to that opinion, the panel laid the blame for this crisis almost exclusively in the lap of American teachers, who were unqualified, lazy, and incompetent.

Commission after commission has since followed in the footsteps of this first group, so that America's teachers are now viewed as a second-class group of intellectually inferior citizens. The result is that many talented young people turn away from careers in education because they understandably have no desire to be seen as stupid, lazy, or the root cause of our society's many ills.

It would be nice if these commissions might once realize that education does not occur in a vacuum. I personally know many deeply qualified and utterly committed educators who work in areas that are not conducive to education. A teacher can work himself nearly to death to impart romance to his students, but if those students come to class hungry the results may not be stellar.

A child's test scores might well be adversely affected if that child spends the day in a classroom where the plaster is caving and the roof is falling in.

A student's GPA might be weakened if that child spends the morning caring for a parent who has been strung out all night. It may be difficult for a student to commit to learning his ABCs when his top priority is not to get gunned down by an assault rifle on the way to school.

A teacher can, and many do, struggle to teach a child to love language when that child comes from a home where the television is a ubiquitous presence and books are never opened. It would be wonderful if just one politician would stand up and say that parents bear *at least* as much responsibility as teachers for our nation's troubled youth. But that kind of courage is almost entirely missing from our political discourse, and so pre-service teachers and new teachers are left to inherit a vocation that is truly under siege and at risk.

Throughout this book, it has been my intention to provide new teachers with the tools necessary to allow you to survive the pitfalls of teaching, so that you may thrive in the promise of teaching. It is so easy to get uselessly bogged down in the petty politics of education, or to become disenchanted with the entire profession because of poor working relationships with an administrator. Our challenge is to remember that education is always about the kids—they are our focus and our responsibility. It is from them that we can draw energy and remind ourselves why we chose this wonderful profession in the first place.

Teaching is a calling. It is a job that requires the greatest commitment and idealism and hope. In the face of those, like the blue ribbon commission types, who would degrade what we do, every educator must have a deep and abiding faith in themselves and their students. Yes, there are poor teachers out there. But I imagine if one put together a blue ribbon panel we could find that there are a few corrupt politicians in our nation, too. That does not mean that public service is a failed notion.

In the Gospel of Luke, chapter twelve, it is written that "from everyone who has been given much, much will be demanded; and from the one who has been entrusted with much, much more will be asked." That is the essence of teaching in America. Being a teacher is about compassion; it is about idealism. It is about demanding the highest moral character and integrity from yourself and your students. It is about challenging yourself each and every day to do and to be better, knowing that your own efforts may change a life, may spark an imagination, may save a smile.

There is another old saying that is often applied to teaching. It says, "Those who can, do; those who can't teach." Ouch. But despite what you may think, I agree with this statement 100 percent. If you cannot sit passively on the sidelines and watch life pass a child by—you teach. If you cannot accept that mediocrity is the way of the world—you teach.

If you cannot believe that there is nothing redeeming in our nation's young—you teach. You may not be told this in your teacher preparation programs, but to be a truly great teacher, it's not how much you know that really matters; it's how much you care. In his autobiography, Gandhi wrote, "My idea was never to entrust children to commonplace teachers. Their literary qualification was not so essential as their moral fibre."[20]

This world belongs to the young. History is molded by the courage, the passion, and the romance of youth. It is shaped by what Robert Kennedy called "the appetite of adventure over the love of ease."[21] There are young people in this nation who suffer. There is the oppression of ignorance and the crime of poverty. There are young people bitter beyond their years, and elders who have been callously discarded by those who stand to learn the most from them. A teacher is given the opportunity to make a difference in the life of a child, and to those given such a majestic chance, much is expected.

When the tide of injustice and inequality threatens to overwhelm you, hold fast to your ideals. When the winds of change rattle your windows, cling to your own good sense. When they tell you that you can't do it—whatever "it" may be—determine to work harder. When they tell you that you are in over your head, determine to swim faster.

In South Africa in 1966, Robert F. Kennedy said,

> Each time a man stands up for an ideal, or acts to improve the lot of others, or strikes out against injustice, he sends forth a tiny ripple of hope; and crossing each other from a million different centers of energy and daring, those ripples build a current which can sweep down the mightiest walls of oppression and resistance.[22]

This is the work of a teacher.

You will grow tired. In 1848, Electa Lincoln, herself a dedicated teacher, lamented, "I am discouraged. Everything seems to go wrong. I do not teach to suit myself. I do not inspire others with zeal, with the deep, lively interest which they should have in their studies. It seems to me," she concluded, "as if I had lost my faculties for teaching, if I ever had them."[23] Every teacher can relate. You are not alone.

Freire unapologetically believed that an important part of a teacher's vocation was working toward utopia—a more equal, compassionate, and just society. He wrote, "Our utopia, our sane insanity, is the creation of a world where power is based on ethics. Without it, the world crumbles and cannot survive."[24] Ever the idealist, Freire was also deeply pragmatic about what it would take to bring about such a society. "Just dreaming of this, however," he wrote, "will not make it concrete. We need to fight unceasingly to build it."[25]

In 1865, forty-eight dedicated abolitionists believed their struggle was over, and that equality had come through what Lincoln called the awful scourge of war. They were, tragically, wrong. As teachers we must remind ourselves every single day that our work is never done, the struggle never fully won. We must never, ever cease believing in the promise and the potential inherent in our—yes, *sacred*—vocation. And, truly, we must fight unceasingly to build a tomorrow worthy of our students.

Notes

1. David W. Blight, *Frederick Douglass: Prophet of Freedom* (New York: Simon and Schuster, 2018), p. 468.

2. Blight, *Frederick Douglas*, p. 469.

3. Samuel L. Blumenfeld, "Foreword." In R. J. Rushdoony, *The Messianic Character of American Education* (Vallecito, CA: Ross House Books, 1963), p. 7.

4. Rushdoony, *The Messianic Character*, p. 43.

5. Rushdoony, *The Messianic Character*, p. 43.

6. John Dewey, *The School and Society and the Child and the Curriculum* (Digireads.com Publishing, 2010), p. 35.

7. Kristina Rizga, "Betsy DeVos Wants to Use America's Schools to Build 'God's Kingdom.'" *Mother Jones*, March/April 2017 issue. Retrieved from https://www.motherjones.com/politics/2017/01/betsy-devos-christian-schools-vouchers-charter-education-secretary/, September 17, 2020.

8. Rizga, "Betsy DeVos Wants to Use America's Schools to Build 'God's Kingdom.'"

9. Valerie Strauss, "She's a Billionaire Who said Schools Need Guns to Fight Bears: Here's What You may not know about Betsy DeVos." *The Washington Post*, February 7, 2017. Retrieved from https://www.washingtonpost.com/news/answer-sheet/wp/2017/02/07/shes-a-billionaire-who-said-schools-need-guns-to-fight-bears-heres-what-you-may-not-know-about-betsy-devos/, September 17, 2020.

10. Chris McGreal, "About 13m US Children Are Living below the Poverty Line, Rights Group Reveals." *The Guardian*, April 30, 2019. Retrieved from https://www.theguardian.com/law/2019/apr/30/us-children-poverty-childrens-defense-fund-report, July 14, 2020.

11. Ronald E. Butchart, *Schooling the Freed People: Teaching, Learning, and the Struggle for Black Freedom, 1861-1876*. (Chapel Hill, NC: University of North Carolina Press, 2010), p. 46.

12. Butchart, *Schooling the Freed People*, p. 69.

13. Nancy MacLean, *Democracy in Chains: The Deep History of the Radical Right's Stealth Plan for America* (New York: Viking, 2017), p. 13.

14. Paulo Freire, *Pedagogy of Freedom: Ethics, Democracy, and Civic Courage* (Lanham, MD: Rowman and Littlefield, 1998), p. 63.

15. MacLean, *Democracy in Chains*, p. 13.

16. James T. Patterson, *Brown v. Board of Education: A Civil Rights Milestone and Its Troubled Legacy* (Oxford: Oxford University Press, 2001), p. 27.

17. Patterson, *Brown v. Board of Education*, p. 27.

18. MacLean, *Democracy in Chains*, p. 13.

19. MacLean, *Democracy in Chains*, p. 13.

20. Mohandas K. Gandhi, *An Autobiography: The Story of My Experiments with the Truth* (Boston, MA: Beacon Press, 1957), p. 420.

21. Maxwell Taylor Kennedy, Ed., *Make Gentle the Life of this World: The Vision of Robert F. Kennedy* (New York: Harcourt Brace, 1998), p. 82.

22. Kennedy, Ed., *Make Gentle the Life of this World*, p. 131.

23. Johann N. Neem, *Democracy's Schools: The Rise of Public Education in America* (Baltimore, MD: Johns Hopkins University Press, 2017), location 2483, Kindle edition.

24. Paulo Freire, *Letters to Cristina: Reflections on My Life and Work* (New York: Routledge, 1996), p. 185.

25. Freire, *Letters to Cristina*, p. 186.

Bibliography

Print

Addams, Jane. *On Education*. London: Transaction Publishers, 2002.
Allen, James. *As a Man Thinketh*. Public Domain.
Andersen, Kurt. *Fantasyland: How America Went Haywire, A 500-Year History*. New York: Random House, 2017.
Ayers, William. *To Teach: The Journey of a Teacher*. New York: Teachers College Press, 1993.
Banks, Dennis with Richard Erdoes. *Ojibwa Warrior: Dennis Banks and the Rise of the American Indian Movement*. Norman, OK: University of Oklahoma Press, 2004.
Bianculli, David. *Dangerously Funny: The Uncensored Story of the Smothers Brothers Comedy Hour*. New York: Touchstone, 2009.
Blight, David W. *Frederick Douglass: Prophet of Freedom*. New York: Simon and Schuster, 2018.
Boyd, Valerie. *Wrapped In Rainbows: The Life of Zora Neale Hurston*. New York: Scribner, 2003.
Brown, DeNeen L. "In Search of an Uncomfortable Truth." *The Washington Post*, March 22, 2020.
Brown, Les. "TV Weighs using Nixon Tapes; Profanity may Pose a Problem." *New York Times* (1923-Current file); New York, NY [New York, NY] May 15, 1974: 90. Retrieved on July 11, 2020.
Butchart, Ronald E. *Schooling the Freed People: Teaching, Learning, and the Struggle for Black Freedom, 1861-1876*. Chapel Hill, NC: University of North Carolina Press, 2010.
Chaplin, Charles. *My Autobiography*. New York: Simon and Schuster, 1964.
Chomsky, Noam. *Chomsky on Miseducation*, Donaldo Macedo, Ed. Lanham, MD: Rowman & Littlefield, 2000.

Clarke, Thurston. *The Last Campaign: Robert F. Kennedy and 82 Days that Inspired America*. New York: Henry Holt, 2008.
Deloria, Jr., Vine. *Custer Died for Your Sins: An Indian Manifesto*. Norman, OK: University of Oklahoma Press, 1969.
Dewey, John. *Democracy and Education*. New York: The Free Press, 1916.
Dewey, John. *Experience and Education*. New York: Touchstone, 1938.
Dewey, John. *The School and Society and the Child and the Curriculum*. Digireads.com Publishing, 2010.
Douglass, Frederick. *Narrative of the Life of Frederick Douglass, An American Slave*. Boston, MA: Bedford Books, 1993.
DuBois, W.E.B. *The Education of Black People: Ten Critiques, 1906-1960*. Herbert Aptheker, Ed. New York: Monthly Review Press, 1973.
Dunkel, Harold B. *Whitehead on Education*. Columbus, OH: Ohio State University Press, 1965.
Emerson, Ralph Waldo. *Selected Writings of Ralph Waldo Emerson*. New York: The Modern Library, 1992.
Evans, Malcolm D. *Whitehead and Philosophy of Education: The Seamless Coat of Learning*. Amsterdam: Rodopi, 1998.
Fitzgerald, Francis. *The Evangelicals: The Struggle to Shape America*. New York: Simon and Schuster, 2017.
Freire, Paulo. *Letters to Cristina: Reflections on My Life and Work*. New York: Routledge, 1996.
Freire, Paulo. *Pedagogy of Freedom: Ethics, Democracy, and Civic Courage*. Lanham, MD: Rowman and Littlefield, 1998.
Freire, Paulo. *Teachers as Cultural Workers: Letters to those Who Dare Teach*. Boulder, CO: Westview, 1998.
Gandhi, Mohandas K. *An Autobiography: The Story of My Experiments with the Truth*. Boston, MA: Beacon Press, 1957.
Greene, Maxine. *The Teacher as Stranger: Educational Philosophy for the Modern Age*. Belmont, CA: Wadsworth, 1973.
Hansen, David T. *The Call to Teach*. New York: Teachers College Press, 1995.
Hedges, Chris. *American Fascists: The Christian Right and the War on America*. New York: Free Press, 2009.
Horton, Myles. "Introduction." In William Ayers, *To Teach: The Journey of a Teacher*. New York: Teachers College Press, 1993.
Hurston, Zora Neale. *Dust Tracks on a Road*. New York: Harper Perennial, 1942.
Illich, Ivan. *Deschooling Society*. New York: Harper and Row, 1970.
Jackson, John A. *A House on Fire: The Rise and Fall of Philadelphia Soul*. London: Oxford University Press, 2004.
Kennedy, Robert F. *Make Gentle the Life of this World: The Vision of Robert F. Kennedy*, Maxwell Taylor Kennedy, Ed. New York: Harcourt, Brace and Company, 1998.
Khan, Hazrat Inayat. *The Heart of Sufism: Essential Writings of Hazrat Inayat Khan*. Boston, MA: Shambhala, 1999.

Khan, Hazrat Inayat. *Sufi Teachings Book One: The Way of Illumination*. Commodius Vicus, E-Publisher, 2012.

Khan, Hazrat Inayat. *Sufi Teachings Book Two: The Mysticism of Music, Sound and Word*. Commodius Vicus, E-Publisher, 2012.

Khan, Hazrat Inayat. *Sufi Teachings Book Three: The Art of Personality*. Commodius Vicus e-Publisher, 2012.

Khan, Hazrat Inayat. *Sufi Teachings Book Five: Spiritual Liberty*. Commodius Vicus, E-Publisher, 2012.

Kimmel, Michael. *Manhood in America: A Cultural History*. New York: Oxford University Press, 2012.

King, Jr., Martin Luther. *A Testament of Hope: The Essential Writings and Speeches of Martin Luther King, Jr.*, James M. Washington, Ed. New York: HarperOne, 1986.

Klein, Jeff Z. "A Sidekick's Little-known Leading Role." *The New York Times*, September 1, 2013. Sunday, late edition, Section SP; Column 0; Sports Desk, p. 13.

Lakoff, George. *Don't Think of an Elephant: Know Your Values and Frame the Debate*. White River Junction, VT: Chelsea Green Publishing, 2004.

Lakoff, George. *Thinking Points: Communicating Our American Values and Vision*. New York: Farrar, Straus, and Giroux, 2006.

Loewen, James W. *Lies My Teacher Told Me: Everything Your American History Textbook Got Wrong*. New York: Touchstone, 1995.

Macedo, Donaldo. "Introduction." In Paulo Freire, *Pedagogy of the Oppressed*. New York: Continuum, 2000.

MacLean, Nancy. *Democracy in Chains: The Deep History of the Radical Right's Stealth Plan for America*. New York: Viking, 2017.

Marable, Manning. *Malcolm X: A Life of Reinvention*. New York: Viking, 2011.

Marchello, Lindsay and Kari Travis. "UNC Lab Schools Changing Formula for Education." *The Enquirer-Journal* (Monroe, NC). Section News, June 11, 2019.

Martin, Jay. *The Education of John Dewey: A Biography*. New York: Columbia University Press, 2002.

Mayer, Jane. *Dark Money: The Hidden History of the Billionaires behind the Rise of the Radical Right*. New York: Anchor Books, 2017.

McChesney, Robert W. "Introduction." In Noam Chomsky's *Profit Over People: Neoliberalism and Global Order*. New York: Seven Stories Press, 1999.

Mesle, C. Robert. *Process-Relational Philosophy: An Introduction to Alfred North Whithead*. West Conshohocken, PA: Templeton Press, 2008.

N.A. "American Women Victims of Hindu Mysticism." *Idaho Statesman*, February 18, 1912, p. 6.

N.A. *Extraordinary Life and Character of Mary Bateman, the Yorkshire Witch, Twelfth Edition*. Leeds: Davies and Company, 1811.

N.A. "Jay Silverheels, Actor, 62, Dead; Was Tonto in TV 'Lone Ranger.'" *The New York Times*, March 6, 1980; ProQuest Historical Newspapers: *The New York Times*, p. D19.

N.A. "Pittsburgh Here After Stormy Trip," *New York Times*, February 27, 1923, p. 21.

N.A. *Times Daily*, Associated Press. "Real-life Professor Inspires 'Dead Poets' Character." July 10, 1989, 4B.

Neem, Johann N. *Democracy's Schools: The Rise of Public Education in America*. Baltimore, MD: Johns Hopkins University Press, 2017.

Nelson, Pete. *Left for Dead: A Young Man's Search for Justice for the USS Indianapolis*. New York: Delacorte Press, 2002.

Nichol, Gene. *Indecent Assembly: The North Carolina Legislature's Blueprint for the War on Democracy and Equality*. Durham, NC: Blair, 2020.

Niebuhr, Reinhold. *Moral Man and Immoral Society; A Study in Ethics and Politics*. Louisville, KY: Westminster John Knox Press, 1932.

Nordstrom, Kris. *Stymied by Segregation: How Integration can Transform North Carolina Schools and the Lives of Its Students*. Raleigh, NC: North Carolina Justice Center, 2019.

Obama, Barack. *The Audacity of Hope*. New York: Three Rivers Press, 2006.

Palmer, Parker. *Courage to Teach: The Inner Landscape of a Teacher's Life*. San Francisco, CA: Jossey-Bass, 1998.

Palonsky, Stuart B. *900 Shows a Year: A Look at Teaching from a Teacher's Side of the Desk*. New York: Random House, 1986.

Patterson, James T. *Brown v. Board of Education: A Civil Rights Milestone and Its Troubled Legacy*. Oxford: Oxford University Press, 2001.

Perrone, Vito. *Lessons for New Teachers*. Boston, MA: McGraw Hill, 2000.

Perrone Vito. *A Letter to Teachers: Reflections on Schooling and the Art of Teaching*. San Francisco, CA: Jossey-Bass, 1991.

Philbrick, Nathaniel. *Mayflower: A Story of Courage, Community, and War*. New York: Viking, 2006.

Pollock, Constance and Daniel Pollock, Eds. *The Book of Uncommon Prayer*. Dallas, TX: Word Publishing, 1996.

Postman, Neil and Charles Weingartner. *Teaching as a Subversive Activity: A No-holds-barred Assault on Outdated Teaching Methods—with Dramatic and Practical Proposals on How Education can be Made Relevant to Today's World*. New York: Delacorte Press, 1969.

Price, Lucien. *Dialogues of Alfred North Whitehead*. Boston, MA: Nonpareil Book, 1954.

Pullias, Earl V. and James D. Young. *A Teacher Is Many Things*. Bloomington, IN: Indiana University Press, 1968.

Raphael, Ray. *The Teacher's Voice: A Sense of Who We Are*. Portsmouth, NH: Heinemann, 1985.

Rushdoony, R.J. *The Messianic Character of American Education*. Vallecito, CA: Ross House Books, 1963.

Sagan, Carl. *The Demon-Haunted World: Science as a Candle in the Dark*. New York: Ballantine Books, 1996.

Stanton, Doug. *In Harm's Way: The Sinking of the USS Indianapolis and the Extraordinary Story of Its Survivors*. New York: Saint Martin's Paperbacks, 2001.
Wells, Melinda Jane. *Teacher Educators' Conceptions of the Responsibility of Teachers as Moral Educators*. Unpublished doctoral dissertation, Boston University, 1998, dissertation abstract.
Whitehead, Alfred North. *Adventures of Ideas*. New York: The Free Press, 1933.
Whitehead, Alfred North. *The Aims of Education and Other Essays*. New York: The Free Press, 1929.
X., Malcolm, and Alex Haley. *The Autobiography of Malcolm X*. New York: Ballantine Books, 1965.
Zinn, Howard. *The Zinn Reader: Writings on Disobedience and Democracy*. New York: Seven Stories Press, 1997.

Internet Sources

"Americans Believe Teachers Are Underpaid." April 10, 2018. Retrieved from https://www.rasmussenreports.com/public_content/lifestyle/education/americans_believe_teachers_are_underpaid, January 1, 2020.
"Appalachian State University College Portrait: Appalachian Classes and Instructors." Retrieved from http://www.collegeportraits.org/NC/Appalachian/print, May 2, 2020.
"Appalachian State University College Portrait: Experiences with Diverse Groups of People and Ideas." Retrieved from http://www.collegeportraits.org/NC/Appalachian/print, May 2, 2020.
"Appalachian State University College Portrait: Undergraduate Snapshot." Retrieved from http://www.collegeportraits.org/NC/Appalachian/print, May 2, 2020.
"Article 29A: University of North Carolina Laboratory Schools." Retrieved from https://www.ncleg.gov/EnactedLegislation/Statutes/PDF/ByArticle/Chapter_116/Article_29A.pdf, July 9, 2020.
Ball, Billy. "Despite Backing of Legislature and UNC Leaders, Critics Worry NC's Lab School Experiment is Doomed to Failure." *NC Policy Watch*, February 7, 2018. Retrieved from http://www.ncpolicywatch.com/2018/02/07/despite-backing-legislature-unc-leaders-critics-worry-ncs-lab-school-experiment-doomed-failure/, July 9, 2020.
Ballard, Jamie. "45% of Americans Believe that Ghosts and Demons Exist." YouGov. Retrieved from https://today.yougov.com/topics/lifestyle/articles-reports/2019/10/21/paranormal-beliefs-ghosts-demons-poll, April 10, 2020.
Benjamin, Medea. "America Dropped 26,171 Bombs in 2016: What a Bloody End to Obama's Reign." *The Guardian*, January 9, 2017. Retrieved from https://www.theguardian.com/commentisfree/2017/jan/09/america-dropped-26171-bombs-2016-obama-legacy, April 9, 2020.
Bershidsky, Leonid. "Why the Financial Times Has a New Owner." *Bloomberg*, July 24, 2015. Retrieved from https://www.bloomberg.com/opinion/articles/2015-07-24/why-the-financial-times-has-a-new-owner, April 17, 2020.

Cohen, Cathy J., Matthew Fowler, Matthew D. Luttig, Vladimir E. Medenica, and Jon C. Rogowski. "Education in America: The Views of Millennials, A Summary of Key Findings from the first-of-its-kind bimonthly survey of racially and ethnically diverse young adults," p. 4. http://genforwardsurvey.com/assets/uploads/2017/09/GenForward-Education-Report_Final.pdf. Retrieved January 1, 2020.

Collins, Gail. "A Very Pricey Pineapple." *New York Times*, April 27, 2012. Retrieved from https://www.nytimes.com/2012/04/28/opinion/collins-a-very-pricey-pineapple.html, April 17, 2020.

Davis, Owen. "No Test Left Behind." *TPM Features*. N.D. Retrieved from https://talkingpointsmemo.com/features/privatization/four/, April 19, 2020.

De Pinto, Jennifer, Fred Backus, Anthony Salvanto. "Most Americans Say Climate Change Should be Addressed Now—CBS Poll." *CBS News*, September 15, 2019. Retrieved from https://www.cbsnews.com/news/cbs-news-poll-most-americans-say-climate-change-should-be-addressed-now-2019-09-15/, April 10, 2020.

Ernman, Malena. "Malena Ernman on Daughter Greta Thunberg: 'She was slowly disappearing into some kind of darkness'." *The Guardian*, February 23, 2020. Retrieved from https://www.theguardian.com/environment/2020/feb/23/great-thunberg-malena-ernman-our-house-is-on-fire-memoir-extract, February 26, 2020.

Gerhardt, Deborah R. "Pay Our Teachers or Lose Your Job: North Carolina is Pushing Its Best Educators Out. We have to do Something." *Slate*, January 5, 2014. Retrieved from https://slate.com/human-interest/2014/01/north-carolinas-assault-on-teachers-has-to-stop.html, May 2, 2020.

Graham, Ruth. "The Bible that Oozed Oil: A Small Georgia Town, a Prophecy about Donald Trump, and the Story of How a Miracle Fell Apart." *Slate*, February 27, 2020. Retrieved from https://slate.com/human-interest/2020/02/oil-bible-dalton-georgia-trump-prophecy-evangelical-miracle.html, March 19, 2020.

"Honesty/Ethics in Professions." Retrieved from https://news.gallup.com/poll/1654/honesty-ethics-professions.aspx, January 1, 2020.

Kamenetz, Anya. "Pearson's Quest to Cover the Planet in Company-Run Schools." *Wired*, April 12, 2016. Retrieved from https://www.wired.com/2016/04/apec-schools/, April 17, 2020.

Kristof, Nicholas. "Government vs. The people." *Herald-Tribune*, January 21, 2016. Retrieved from https://www.heraldtribune.com/article/LK/20160121/Opinion/605202155/SH/, April 28, 2020.

Leuchtenburg, William. "Behind the Ronald Reagan Myth: 'No one had ever entered the White House so grossly ill informed'." *Salon*, December 28, 2015. Retrieved from https://www.salon.com/2015/12/27/behind_the_ronald_reagan_myth_no_one_had_ever_entered_the_white_house_so_grossly_ill_informed_2/, February 11, 2020.

Lymn, Katherine and Alison Dirr. "Rep. John Lewis to Grads: Get into 'good trouble.'" *USA Today*, June 14, 2015. Retrieved from https://www.usatoday.com/story/news/nation/2015/06/14/rep-john-lewis-to-grads-get-into-good-trouble/71226886/, April 7, 2020.

Madani, Doha. "Possible Mass Grave from 1921 Tulsa Race Massacre Found by Researchers." *NBC News*, December 16, 2019. Retrieved from https://www.nbcnews.com/news/nbcblk/possible-mass-grave-1921-tulsa-race-massacre-found-researchers-n1102781, April 14, 2020.

Mann, William J. "How Marlon Brando Made Hollywood Face Its Racism—at the Oscars." *The Daily Beast*, December 15, 2019. Retrieved from https://www.thedailybeast.com/how-marlon-brando-made-hollywood-face-its-racism-at-the-oscars, March 22, 2020.

McGreal, Chris. "About 13m US Children Are Living below the Poverty Line, Rights Group Reveals." *The Guardian*, April 30, 2019. Retrieved from https://www.theguardian.com/law/2019/apr/30/us-children-poverty-childrens-defense-fund-report, July 14, 2020.

The MetLife Survey of the American Teacher: Challenges for School Leadership. February 2013, p. 6. Retrieved from https://www.metlife.com/content/dam/microsites/about/corporate-profile/MetLife-Teacher-Survey-2012.pdf, January 2, 2020.

Mettler, Katie. "'Good Trouble': How John Lewis Fuses New and Old Tactics to Teach about Civil Disobedience." *The Washington Post*, June 23, 2016. Retrieved from https://www.washingtonpost.com/news/morning-mix/wp/2016/06/23/good-trouble-how-john-lewis-fuses-new-and-old-tactics-to-teach-about-civil-disobedience/, April 7, 2020.

"Middle Fork Elementary School Profile." Retrieved from https://www.schooldigger.com/go/NC/schools/0150002728/school.aspx, July 3, 2020.

National Education Association. 2017 National Education Association Representative Assembly, "NEA Policy Statement on Charter Schools," July 2017. Retrieved from https://ra.nea.org/nea-policy-statement-charter-schools/, May 2, 2020.

Newell, Sarah. "Middle Fork to Partner with App State for School Conversion in 2018-2019." *The Winston Salem Journal*. November 7, 2017. Retrieved from https://www.journalnow.com/news/local/middle-fork-to-partner-with-app-state-for-school-conversion-in-2018-19/article_e8971ced-3412-53f0-bfa8-8ff5d8b322c5.html, May 2, 2020.

Parker, Ryan. "Harrison Ford Once Joked the Studio Executive Who Disliked His First Film Became His Butler." *The Hollywood Reporter*, July 13, 2016. Retrieved from https://www.hollywoodreporter.com/heat-vision/harrison-ford-birthday-star-joked-910573, February 11, 2020.

PDK Poll of the public's attitudes toward the public schools 2019. Retrieved from https://pdkpoll.org/results, January 2, 2020.

"Results from the 2017 Education Next Poll." Retrieved from https://www.educationnext.org/2017-ednext-poll-interactive/, January 1, 2020.

Rizga, Kristina. "Betsy DeVos Wants to Use America's Schools to Build 'God's Kingdom.'" *Mother Jones*, March/April 2017 issue. Retrieved from https://www.motherjones.com/politics/2017/01/betsy-devos-christian-schools-vouchers-charter-education-secretary/, September 17, 2020.

Romo, Vanessa. "New Research Identifies Possible Mass Graves from 1921 Tulsa Race Massacre." National Public Radio, December 17, 2019. Retrieved from https://www.npr.org/2019/12/17/789015343/new-research-identifies-possible-mass-graves-from1921-tulsa-race-massacre, April 14, 2020.

Sidey, Hugh. "The Lesson John Kennedy Learned from the Bay of Pigs." *Time*, April 16, 2001. Retrieved from http://content.time.com/time/nation/article/0,8599,1065 37,00.html, February 11, 2020.

Simon, Stephanie. "No Profit Left Behind: In the High-Stakes World of American Education, Pearson Makes Money Even When Its Results don't Measure Up." *Politico*, February 10, 2015. Retrieved from https://www.politico.com/story/2015/02/pearson-education-115026_Page2.html, April 17, 2020.

Strauss, Valerie. "She's a Billionaire Who Said Schools Need Guns to Fight Bears: Here's What You may not know about Betsy DeVos." *The Washington Post*, February 7, 2017. Retrieved from https://www.washingtonpost.com/news/answer-sheet/wp/2017/02/07/shes-a-billionaire-who-said-schools-need-guns-to-fight-bears-heres-what-you-may-not-know-about-betsy-devos/, September 17, 2020.

Strauss, Valerie. "Why Education Activists Are Furious at ExxonMobil's CEO." *The Washington Post*, December 29, 2015. Retrieved from https://www.washingtonpost.com/news/answer-sheet/wp/2015/12/27/why-education-activists-are-furious-at-exxonmobils-ceo/, April 29, 2020.

Tarnoff, Ben. "Neoliberalism Turned Our World into a Business: And there Are Two Big Winners." *The Guardian*, December 13, 2016. Retrieved from https://www.theguardian.com/us-news/2016/dec/13/donald-trump-silicon-valley-leaders-neoliberalism-administration, April 17, 2020.

Thomas, Dexter. "Q&A: Meet the Woman Who Refused Marlon Brando's Oscar and Inspired Jada Pinkett Smith's Boycott." *Los Angeles Times*, February 5, 2016. Retrieved from https://www.latimes.com/entertainment/movies/moviesnow/la-et-mn-sacheen-littlefeather-oscars-20160204-htmlstory.html, March 22, 2020.

Vaidyanathan, Gayathri. "Big Gap between What Scientists Say and Americans Think about Climate Change: But the Gap may be Closing between Scientists and the Public on Global Warming." *Scientific American*, January 30, 2015. Retrieved from https://www.scientificamerican.com/article/big-gap-between-what-scientists-say-and-americans-think-about-climate-change/, April 10, 2020.

Wilson, John. "The Most Backward Legislature in America." *Education Week*, July 29, 2013. Retrieved from http://blogs.edweek.org/edweek/john_wilson_unleashed/2013/07/the_most_backward_legislature_in_america.html, May 2, 2020.

"Winston Salem State University College Portrait: Undergraduate Snapshot." Retrieved from http://www.collegeportraits.org/NC/WSSU/print, May 2, 2020.

www.ingramcontent.com/pod-product-compliance
Lightning Source LLC
Chambersburg PA
CBHW020748230426
43665CB00009B/532